Husband and wife team W~~illi~~ ~~and Abigail~~ run
many succes~~s~~ful pop-up
well as a pop-up food ~~/~~ing
previous~~l~~y worked as a hea ~~ster~~
and London, William spec ~~~~ and
his wife shoot themselves. Former national magazine editor
Abigail has previously worked as a restaurant critic and launched
a successful food magazine. William and Abigail run a popular
cookery blog called The Shotgun Chef, which was nominated
for the National Blog Awards and they currently run a pop-up
cookery school in Scotland.

Also published by Constable & Robinson

The Easy eBay Business Guide

Fundraising Ideas

How To Make Money at Car Boot Sales

The Small Business Start-up Workbook

Start and Run a Business from Home

How to Make Sales When You Don't Like Selling

HOW TO RUN A POP-UP RESTAURANT

Abigail and William Alldis

A HOW TO BOOK

ROBINSON

ROBINSON

First published in Great Britain in 2015 by Robinson

A CIP catalogue record for this book
is available from the British Library.

ISBN 978-1-47211-908-7 (paperback)
ISBN: 978-1-47211-909-4 (ebook)

Typeset in by Basement Press, Glaisdale, UK.
Printed and bound in Great Britain by Clays Ltd, St Ives plc
Papers used by Robinson are from well-managed forests and other responsible sources

MIX
Paper from
responsible sources
FSC® C104740

Robinson
is an imprint of
Little, Brown Book Group
Carmelite House
50 Victoria Embankment
London EC4Y 0DZ

An Hachette UK Company
www.hachette.co.uk

www.littlebrown.co.uk

How To Books are published by Constable & Robinson, a part of Little, Brown
Book Group. We welcome proposals from authors who have first-hand experience
of their subjects. Please set out the aims of your book, its target market and its
suggested contents in an email to Nikki.Read@howtobooks.co.uk

CONTENTS

PREFACE

I must confess, I thought my husband was completely insane when he suggested, a month into our marriage, that we should run a pop-up restaurant from our front room to run alongside our cookery blog The Shotgun Chef. We were living in a small former fishing village in Essex in a ramshackle, yet charming, sixteenth-century cottage on Wivenhoe High Street. I conceded that our home was well situated to attract passing customers, being next to a pub and on the busiest street in the town, but our home was certainly not equipped with a commercial kitchen, had only one downstairs toilet and, as the cottage had been a former bakery, had what could only be described as a 'quirky' layout.

Initial worries

And it wasn't just the venue that concerned me. My mind anxiously started racing with the technicalities: was it legal to set up this small business in our front room? What about health and safety? What if things went wrong on the night and customers wanted their money back? Were we even capable of serving three courses to sixteen people at once from our tiny, one-person kitchen?

The stupid thing is I'd been quite happily hosting dinner parties for up to ten people for most of my adult life, and these issues had never crossed my mind. It was simply that the use of the professional term 'restaurant' had struck fear into my very (practical) soul.

My husband, being an optimistic sort of fellow, calmed my fears. He explained that he'd happily been running such events years before we'd met, and that recent legislation had been brought in to allow small businesses to run commercial ventures in empty spaces and temporarily sell alcohol. Our front room being empty, he had concluded, qualified us perfectly. Everything would be fine, he assured me.

And so, nervously, I agreed. We carefully selected our menu – all seasonal, fresh and local produce. It being autumn and my husband coming from a farming background, we decided to theme our restaurant around game, to try and educate the village about this somewhat mystical foodstuff. We made sure there was a vegetarian menu option too, so as not to alienate any of the village. We put a poster in our front window, advertising three courses for £28, with details about the food, and half a bottle of wine thrown in for free. Two weeks before the event we were fully booked. People had emailed us their menu choices and dropped a cheque through the door in advance, so we didn't have to have any conversations about money on the night.

Opening night

Two hours before our guests' arrival I was running around the house screaming like a banshee about the state of the place: why weren't there fresh guest soaps in the downstairs loo? Why weren't the glasses properly polished? Where had the Hoover gone? I'd lapsed into 'entertaining meltdown'. My husband shooed me out of the kitchen and upstairs to have a bath, glass of wine, and calm my restaurant-crazed self down. By the time I came back downstairs, dressed to impress, he'd cleaned down the kitchen, finished his prep, got the wine on ice, was playing smooth jazz on the iPad and was busily lighting the 4,000 tealights I'd dotted around our home to create just the right fuzzy glowing atmosphere. 'Wine?' he suggested, and topped up my glass. It was then that I realised, I'd forgotten the most important ingredient of the whole evening – to actually enjoy it. As soon as the first guests arrived, I clicked into hostess mode and the evening flew by. We'd staggered our guests by 15 minutes each, but due to early and late arrivals, people pretty much turned up all together. I started to panic again. 'Don't worry,' said my husband, 'It will be fine.' And so it was. Some courses went out later than I'd have liked, some more quickly than I thought elegant. Some dishes surpassed expectations and my service was, on the whole, attentive, except for the occasional moment when I got distracted trying to micromanage the kitchen. And when I stepped back, I noticed customers were happy to be in our cosy, candlelit home, nosing around, enjoying conversations with the other guests and my husband's somewhat sublime food. Despite my initial panic, it didn't take long for me to relax in front of guests and put on a cool, calm and collected front.

Bolstered by success

A few customers were surprised they had to sit with strangers – due to space restrictions we had to have tables of four – but by the end of the evening these initial strangers had become firm friends. Others decided they didn't like where they were seated and so moved to different tables, which meant their orders were momentarily muddled up, but people were patient and kind and everyone left with full bellies, praise for the chef and wrapped us up in grand hugs and kisses, promising to return for our next event. As indeed they did, bringing friends and family with them. And the brimming cash pot after tips had been thrown in made us hungry for more supper club and pop-up restaurant success.

We've learnt a lot since that first evening. With hindsight, it was more of a very formal supper club than a pop-up restaurant in the strictest sense, and our events have grown in size and ambition as our confidence has flourished. Yes, we've made mistakes: such as freezing the wine and then having to defrost it over the radiator; or asking inexperienced friends to help run a cocktail bar, which ensured a good time was had by all but their generous measures ate heavily into our profits. But every experience has been a learning curve, and we've picked up some fantastic tips along the way that we'd like to share with you so you can be sure of success on your first night.

We now know:

- How to plan a low-labour menu, mixing hot, cold and ready-prepped courses to take the pressure off the kitchen staff.
- How to increase our income with a Temporary Events Notice.
- How to get all the right insurance and paperwork in place, and tick all the health and safety boxes.
- How to quickly fix the most common restaurateur's problems, with a few simple-to-follow rules.

Tips from the pros

William and I have spoken to some of the country's leading pop-up restaurateurs and supper club hosts, alongside fresh-faced amateurs and pop-up critics, whose insights, along with our own experiences, will help you hold your first lip-smackingly successful event that will turn your passion for food into profit. So read on for more amusing anecdotes and tips from the pros, alongside guidelines on your legal responsibilities, inspiration on how to pick your theme and find your perfect venue, budget for success, conquer online marketing, tap into funding and maximise your profit so you can kick-start your own utterly successful pop-up restaurant or supper club, and give the *MasterChef* finalists a run for their money!

Abigail Alldis

INTRODUCTION

How to use this book

In this book, we show you how to come up with the vision for your pop-up restaurant or supper club, plan your evening, publicise it and finally hold your own successful event. We'll advise on everything from budgets to staffing, to how to deal with the paperwork and ensure everything about your evening is legal.

We're assuming if you've picked up this book, you're already passionate about food, and you also want to use it to help generate an income (or at least cover the costs of holding a great night). You could be wanting to use a pop-up to promote a foodstuff such as cheese or fantastic ales that you currently make; or you might be a chef and want to see if you're ready to open your own restaurant; or a keen amateur considering a career change. Perhaps you are one of a group of chefs who fancy a short-term collaboration; or are simply someone who enjoys cooking and is hoping to hold occasional events in your own home to bring in some extra income. Whatever your motivation, this book should answer all your questions and guide you smoothly past the pitfalls of holding your own pop-up restaurant or supper club.

Planning your event

Early on in this book we look at how to discover the demand for a pop-up restaurant or supper club in your area, and how to come up with the concept for your eatery in general. This involves everything from deciding what kind of food you want to provide, what the price point will be, how you're going to theme your evening, picking a venue and being realistic about what you can achieve on the night.

Making it happen

We look at the more practical aspects of turning your dream into a reality. This involves staffing the evening, filling in all the paperwork and taking care of the legal requirements, how to finance your venture, negotiate over venues, and source props and table dressings.

Finding your customers

Publicity and marketing are absolutely essential if you want to make sure that people actually attend. We'll help you to come up with a media strategy and look at everything from how to target your customers to actually getting them through the door. We'll show you how to use social media and blogs effectively for a longer-term marketing strategy, how to tap into the local press and specialist publications, how to use various communities to market your venture, and how to approach more traditional marketing methods such as flyers and posters to guarantee success. We focus on brand awareness and ensuring the message you're sending out before the big night gives your evening the biggest chance of success.

Holding your night

We count down your final few days until opening and help you to ensure everything is in place to run a stress-free night. We take you step by step through your evening and provide plenty of case studies, so you can learn from the successes and mistakes of other professional pop-up restaurateurs and supper club hosts. We also look at what the best in the business consider are important features in running a successful restaurant so you can incorporate some of their ideas and advice into your evening, alongside some excellent recovery strategies if things get out of hand.

Where to go from here

This is an often-overlooked part of running pop-up restaurants – but is essential if you want to actually grow your event and hold more in the future. We show you how to review how your night went, gather useful feedback from customers, learn from your mistakes and build on the success and momentum to develop your pop-up restaurant in the future. We've also included contact details for some useful organisations that we've found invaluable when planning and growing our pop-up restaurants.

Adapting the advice to your own needs

Please feel free to dip in and out of chapters as you begin the journey of planning your pop-up restaurant or supper club, and adapt the advice given to suit your specific ideas. The timeframes and order of organising things aren't set in stone, but this is what we found easiest (although every evening we've held has been unique in its own wonderful way).

Good luck!

William and Abigail Alldis

CHAPTER 1
WHY RUN A POP-UP RESTAURANT OR SUPPER CLUB?

What are pop-ups?

The whole pop-up scene has exploded in the past five years, with everything from pop-up theatres, pop-up boutiques and pop-up cafés now accepted as legitimate businesses on the high street. They usually involve taking over an unused or unusual space for a short period of time and offer a quirky experience that is out of the ordinary. This makes pop-ups fantastic when combined with food or drink, as these are worlds in which tastes and fashions are constantly changing; and with something as creative as cooking or mixology (that's cocktail making to you and I), you really can let your imagination run free!

Flexible and low risk

The concept is fantastic for testing the market for a new restaurant in your local area, giving you instant feedback on the popularity of your style of cooking without massive start-up costs. If you're passionate about food but also short of cash, a pop-up can give you the flexibility to hold on to your full-time job, so you can see if a career in cooking is for you.

Pop-ups are also much easier to organise now than ever before, with many venues lying empty post-recession, and new legislation making it simple for you to take over spaces and hold events, as long as they are for a short period of time (perfect for a pop-up restaurant!). The key thing to remember is that to take advantage of this new legislation your supper club or restaurant must be temporary – even if you are planning to expand it to a more permanent venture in the future. Keeping this in mind will help you to stay true to the spirit of the pop-up restaurant or supper club vibe, meaning you will stay creative, adaptable and exciting along the way.

Pop-up and supper club: what's the difference?

The terms 'supper club' and 'pop-up restaurant' are often used interchangeably, but there's a subtle difference between them that means diners' expectations will be different, and your approach to running each will vary too.

With a supper club, the setting is usually fairly informal and it will often take place in the host's home. Your guests will sit down together and be served either a set menu or a tasting menu consisting of many courses. Often your guests will be asked to bring their own alcohol to get around licensing issues and news of your evening will usually be spread by word of mouth, although some websites such as www.thelondonfoodie.co.uk and www.supperclubfangroup.ning.com will list upcoming events. The courses are served in one sitting and many chefs sit down to eat with their guests.

Pop-up restaurants

With a pop-up restaurant, however, the expectations are different. Your customers will anticipate a more professional quality of service, an evening with slightly more finesse, and they will want to choose their food. They will also expect to sit with their companions and be able to book a table for a certain time. Pop-up restaurants can usually charge more for these evenings and, if they have applied for a Temporary Events Notice, will sell wine. The supper club is more about the food, whereas the pop-up restaurant is also about theatre.

Which one should I run?

Think about what it is you want to achieve and what you think you are able to pull off, without being overwhelmed. If your food and location is more suited to an informal group sit-down, then don't force it into something it is not. If you would prefer to concentrate on cooking good food, rather than excelling at service or hunting for a theatrical venue, then it's likely a supper club is more suitable. Also look at your skill set – if you don't have a background in professional cooking, marketing or front-of-house service and have no one to help you with any of these, you may find a pop-up restaurant will be a baptism of fire. In this case, start smaller with a supper club and as your experience grows, so too will your skill set. The lines between the two types of events can be somewhat blurred, but the clue for what people will expect is in the title. For example, our Valentine's Day Pop-Up Speakeasy was clearly going to involve a well-stocked cocktail bar, big-band tunes, slightly chaotic service and dancing on tables!

Organic growth

The beauty of starting a supper club, pop-up restaurant or indeed any other pop-up business, is that you don't have to spend months planning. The spirit of the pop-up celebrates adaptability and functions as a work in progress. They grow organically, in response to the experiences of the proprietor, and because they are light in paperwork, red tape, set-up costs and responsibility, you can get on with what you really love doing – cooking food and entertaining people.

You can get your restaurant up and running, and test and refine it using real customers' feedback, instead of planning every minute detail in the run-up to launch day. Some people will find this daunting, but for most creative types it's the way they love working best.

Seizing opportunities

A pop-up restaurant allows you to grasp opportunities quickly: such as a fantastic temporary venue coming on to the market; discovering a certain type of ingredient in abundance; meeting a group of people who want to throw their energy and enthusiasm behind you; or perhaps a local village restaurant is closed for a fortnight while the owners go on holiday – this is your chance to fill that gap in the market.

It also means you are able to change your plans quickly to adapt to circumstances that arise. All this makes the pop-up model of business perfect for up-and-coming chefs, most of whom thrive in a creative, unrestrictive environment.

Stick to your aim

Don't lose sight of why you are holding your event. Is it to showcase your cookery talents to friends and family? To test the market with the aim of launching your own restaurant? To share the love of an unusual cuisine you have discovered? Or to generate an income?

Let this driving factor dictate your decisions and it will help to ensure you achieve this. When you're clear about what your aim is, you will know whether a supper club or a pop-up restaurant is for you.

Deciding which one you should run

Pros of pop-up restaurants over supper clubs

- A Temporary Events Notice allows you to hold up to twelve events a year without being subject to business rates – so it's a quick and easy way of generating cash if you find a friendly landlord.

- You could look at taking over a local restaurant on a quiet night, so you have a fully set-up kitchen and trained staff without the inconvenience of having strangers in your home.
- It's also a fantastic way of testing your market if you plan to eventually open a full-time restaurant, and get genuine customer feedback, without outlaying big money on the risk of a full-time business. And, if you're hoping for some regular income from your restaurant, and you're trialling it as a more regular eaterie, if you find you're getting repeat customers, you know you're on to something.
- Using the term 'restaurant' allows you to charge more for your food.

Pros of supper clubs over pop-up restaurants

- A supper club is a more relaxed affair – you can get away with a more informal service and focus on just the food.
- People attend a supper club with a very open mind – they are happy to taste new foods. At a pop-up restaurant expectations are likely to be higher, and won't just involve the food, but the service, venue and table dressings: the whole package.
- Guests at a supper club will generally be sought through family and friends, so there is a safety net, whereas pop-up restaurants will usually be attended by strangers. Many people comfortably start out by running a supper club and then, if successful, bump it up to restaurant status. You don't need to bite off more than you can chew.
- There are fewer financial responsibilities attached to running a supper club, such as rent and an alcohol licence, and many of your utility bills will be absorbed into your everyday living costs.

Can I really do that?

The pop-up restaurant or bar is nothing new – you've probably even been to one yourself without knowing it. Fundraising lunches in the local village hall, or a mulled wine stall at a Christmas market are examples of old-school pop-up restaurant or bar ventures. However, in recent years these have turned into commercial enterprises, with a professional level of food and service, and there is something quite spectacular about them. When guests visit a pop-up, they're expecting something fantastical, something out of the ordinary, so you need to let your imagination run free.

The good news is if you've ever cooked for someone else and received favourable reviews, then you're capable of holding a supper club. At the heart of a successful restaurant or supper club is great food: no amount of marketing hype will change that. And if the food is great and your pricing's right, there is, in theory, nothing that will keep people from your door. But word-of-mouth recommendations take time to spread, and with a pop-up restaurant you really need to hit the ground running as you will have the outlay of rent, staffing, venue dressings, insurances and ingredients to meet to break even.

Simple pleasures

Of course, all those other elements help: fantastic service, wow-factor decor and good quality restaurant dressings will all boost the dining experience and help make your night the Shangri-La of eateries. But often it is the simple, well-cooked meals, served in warm, friendly surroundings that we remember best. One of our fondest dinner memories is of a fresh lobster in garlic butter with a cold bottle of beer, served in a corrugated tin hut on a beach in St Lucia for two dollars. The paper plate, chequered tablecloth and honking of horns from the gridlocked road of jeeps in front did nothing to detract from the fact that this was the fleshiest, freshest and meatiest lobster that has ever scuttled across the face of this Earth. Many £300 meals with views from the Gherkin and five-star service have yet to give that dinner a run for its money.

Other reasons to 'pop up'

Pop-ups aren't only an opportunity for budding chefs – they are a way of presenting products in an unusual and exciting format. Food and drink PR company R&R Teamwork collaborate with already successful chefs to put on exciting events that celebrate the brands they represent, such as pop-up pork scratching banquets and beer-tasting evenings.

Be inspired!

Think about the local suppliers in your area who may be willing to team up with you and help promote your evening: could you do a ten-course tasting menu celebrating local cheeses? Or a seafood tasting menu of local oysters, mussels, crab, mackerel and bass? Join forces with a local chocolatier for an evening travelling throughout the history of this delicious foodstuff; or explore how it is used around the world – the Incas were big fans of chocolate and often paired it with chilli (think chocolate chilli con carne). Take inspiration from anywhere and everywhere.

CASE STUDY
POP-UP RESTAURANT AS PUBLICITY FOR A PRODUCT

Heston Blumenthal, owner of the critically acclaimed Fat Duck restaurant was tasked with creating an Olympics-themed menu for British Airways during London 2012. As part of the publicity, punters were able to sample the menus from a pop-up restaurant in Shoreditch, east London, before the meals were available on board the planes. This created a buzz around the collaboration and gave a fantastic story that everyone, not just those who were flying with BA, could get involved with: one of the world's leading chefs takes on one of the world's worst meals – come along and judge for yourselves. PR doesn't get much more juicy than that!

CHAPTER 2
PLANNING AND RESEARCH

Planning your pop up may seem dull when you just want to get your teeth into putting on your event, but this part of the process is the way you iron out problems and pitfalls before you make them – don't shy away from it!

Doing your research

The first stage you need to go through, before the exciting task of picking your theme, is doing your research to identify gaps in the market. This may seem super-boring, but trust us – put the hard work in here and you will save yourself plenty of embarrassment later on. After all, there's no point trying to market the world's finest tapas restaurant if there are three other fantastic Spanish restaurants half empty in your area. Remember, the pop-up restaurant and supper club ethos is that you do something extraordinary to drum up excitement, so you need to make sure that's what your restaurant will do.

Find out what other food is on offer locally. Speak to people in the street, read the work of or even interview local food critics or food magazine journalists. Speak to other chefs and put questions out on local online forums: what's going on in the food scene in your area? What are others doing well and what's missing? Which restaurants have recently opened (and closed), and if they've failed, why?

Have there been any other pop-up restaurants or supper clubs nearby? How did they do? If they didn't succeed, why was this? Was it the location? Resistance from local customers to the idea?

Lack of publicity? Unpopular food? Finding out all these things in advance will give you a good understanding of the climate in which your food will be received – big-city foodies are very pop-up restaurant and supper club savvy, but their expectations will be high, and there's plenty of competition for their custom. Smaller villages may be wary of a pop-up restaurant or supper club venture, but also more restricted in the number of eateries on offer, so here you will have a captive market. You will need to tap into the feelings of your potential customers and pitch your eatery to meet their needs (after all, there's no point having a restaurant or supper club if you have no customers!).

Learning from others

Research will also mean that you avoid the past pitfalls others have stumbled into. Visit other pop-up restaurants, see what they are doing well and think about what you would improve. This may mean a visit to a bigger city, but it's worth it because you will learn bucketloads. Ask to speak to the people running them – most of them will be happy to give advice as they understand the excitement (and trepidation) involved in launching your own pop-up food adventure. Pick the brains of staff serving you on the evening. Look at the restaurant's marketing material, website, Twitter feeds and blogs – see what they're doing well, and then use that to inspire you. If they're giving off an unprofessional vibe, ask yourself why? What is it they're doing wrong? If their food seems overpriced, again, think how you'd do it differently – what would make it more appealing? You may be impatient to get things off the ground, but this research is training your brain to be able to spot opportunities and make smart decisions when it comes to setting up on your own.

Supper club and pop-up research online

There are several online resources you can use to discover what is out there, and pop-up restaurateurs and supper clubs are huge in the blogging world.

TOP TIP

GET BLOGGING

We started out blogging about the meals we were cooking in our kitchen on a simple WordPress site and one year on theshotgunchef.co.uk had more than 7,000 followers! This was a vital tool for us when trying to promote our supper clubs and pop-up restaurants further down the line.

The best foodie blogsites

Take a look at our pick of some of the best pop-up food blogs out there:

- www.londonpopups.com – An interesting resource that includes not only pop-up restaurants and supper clubs, but also pop-up bars and any other pop-up ventures in London, complete with maps to help you find them.
- www.twentysomethinglondon.com – A site that celebrates the independent side of London – places, events and general quirky happenings.
- www.squaremeal.co.uk – Gives the lowdown on the food scene, including pop-ups, across the country.
- www.hot-dinners.com – Get the insider knowledge on what's happening on the London food scene, including reviews from Britain's most respected food critics.
- www.supperclubfangroup.ning.com – You've guessed it; for details on supper clubs nationwide.

- www.thehandbook.com – This website has its finger on the pulse of London's pop-up restaurant scene.
- www.thenudge.com – The Nudge has a dedicated section dealing with pop-ups in the London area.
- www.londonstreetfoodie.co.uk – Run by the Evening Standard food editor Victoria Stewart this site tracks down the best of London's street food. With carts, trucks and vans 'popping up' all across the capital – part of the fun is trying to find them before they disappear.

These sites may be mainly for London, but this will give you some inspiration as to what is going on out there in the pop-up restaurant scene. Remember, translate this information to where you're pitching your pop-up – what are the needs of your customers? What's happening on top of the London Eye might not be what's needed in your community.

Twitter

Twitter is a valuable resource for finding information about supper clubs and pop-up restaurants, thanks to its immediate and transitory nature. Try using hashtags such as #popuprestaurant, #popup and #foodie.

Identifying elements for success

There are several elements that will guarantee your pop-up restaurant or supper club is a success, and if you neglect any of them, it's likely your foodie venture will flounder. The good news is, pay attention to getting these right and the rest of your planning, preparation and launch night will fall neatly into place.

Write notes on each of the following elements and have a clear idea of what you want to achieve in each area, and how you are going to make that happen.

1. Good food

All chefs will tell you that using top-quality raw ingredients means you have a much higher chance of delivering a delicious dish (and the less you will have to do to those ingredients to get them there). This doesn't necessarily mean you have to spend thousands of pounds on foie gras or oysters, but if you're opening a pop-up chip shop make sure yours are the best chips in town – from the finest potatoes, fried crisp to perfection. If that means spending a few pence more on fresher, seasonal, more suitable potatoes, then so be it. Practise your recipes over and over again, so that on the night you could churn out those dishes in your sleep, meaning they will be foolproof when you're under pressure. Good food spreads by word of mouth fast – get this right, and your other jobs just became a whole lot easier.

2. Opening on the right days

Look at when people in your area are most likely to go out for food. Work out what other local eateries are doing and try to complement them. Is there a gap in the market? Is one of the nearby restaurants closed while people go on holiday? In our village, we knew that the local café was shut on New Year's Day, so we opened a pop-up diner to dish up New Year's morning fry-ups (at a premium price!) – look for opportunities and exploit them.

3. The right location

High streets are great for high footfall, but this also creates a busy, bustling atmosphere; for a pop-up American diner, that's perfect, but for an intimate romantic restaurant, maybe not so much. Remember, the venue in itself can be part of the pop-up restaurant or supper club experience, so having to discover your destination down a hidden alley or on a boat ride across the river could add to the interest, excitement and enjoyment of the evening.

4. The right vibe

How does your restaurant look and feel? Is it cohesive with your theme and your price point? If you have staff, are they treating customers in a way that ties in with the experience you want to create? The way you dress your restaurant, design your menu and display your food all needs to come together like a symphony – not a hotchpotch patchwork of different themes and ideals. This is why the planning stage is so important – keep what you want to achieve tight and focused, and you will know you can deliver a polished, professional night.

5. The right marketing

Most people will have made up their mind about you before they've even walked in the door. That's because your branding, which you create through social media, posters, interviews and blogs, tells everyone who you are. It reveals your identity. Do you want to be seen as lively and upbeat? Sophisticated? Secretive? Cheap and cheerful? Exclusive? Wild and unpredictable? Imagine your pop-up as a person – how would he/she think, act and speak? Then use this to dictate the marketing message you give out.

Involving the community

We also held a pop-up game food shop at our home on the High Street at Christmas time – with everything from game pies to smoked mallard, Christmas turkeys and hot venison burgers on sale – which brought more footfall for all the other businesses in the area. A pop-up local game shop also increased the village's kudos as a sustainable and desirable foodie area, and we were seen as helping to educate people about living off the land. We even gave our services free of charge and put on a fire-pit barbecue in the community garden, as well as providing food for the local ecology group's events – not only because we believed in the project, but also because it is a good way of encouraging the community to embrace what we do.

TOP TIP
THINK LOCAL
- When creating your plan, always be sensitive to the 'local aspect'. How can you help feed back into the community, so you can get their support rather than be looked at as competition? For example, for our pop-up restaurants we always bought the cheeseboard and a few key ingredients from local businesses, and they in turn put in a good word with their customers and hung posters of our menus in their window.
- We found out when local eateries would be closed due to holidays and so on, and asked if they minded if we held an event on those days.
- William also worked as an emergency chef in our village pubs, so we all supported one another, rather than acting as competition. Where we could, we used local fish suppliers, and the local (very talented) baker – fostering goodwill in a tight-knit community is the key to getting that much-needed support when you're starting up.

The perfect ten of planning

Step 1: Plan your pop-up!

Be clear on its purpose and how you will know if you've delivered. You don't necessarily have to work through this plan strictly in this order – for example, you may already have a venue earmarked that you will tweak the food to fit in with, or have your heart set on a theme for the evening, which will dictate your menu. Feel free to customise this plan to suit your own pop-up vision.

- Decide on food.
- Theme.
- Select some possible venues to approach – consider how you will cook in them if they're not already restaurants.
- Will you need staff?
- How many people do you want to invite/cook for?
- How will you seat them all?
- How will you dress the venue?
- Will you sell alcohol?
- Will you market it yourself or employ people to help you?
- Do you need to hire a designer for posters and menus?
- Can you run your own social media account and blog? If not, who can help you?
- Can you take your own photography?
- Do any family or friends possess any of the above skills?
- How much will you need to charge and to how many people to break even?
- Use spreadsheet software to help keep a lid on costs.

Step 2: Approach your venues and book one

You now have your date! Tweak your plan and budget now that you have your venue cost and size, and are aware of the cookery limitations. Factor in whether you will need to hire catering equipment. Decide how people are going to pay you.

Step 3: Apply for your Temporary Events Notice (TEN) if needed

You will need this if you plan to sell alcohol. Decide if you will apply for public liability insurance or if it's already covered through your home insurance. You will need a TEN if you are holding an event in a venue that has not been previously licensed.

Step 4: Book to hire any catering equipment you will need.

You may find that local furniture and kitchen stores are happy to loan you items in exchange for promoting them in interviews and on the night.

Step 5: Start your marketing campaign

Set up a blog, Twitter, Instagram, Pinterest and Facebook accounts; design, print and put up posters, and distribute leaflets; approach supper club and pop-up websites to get your event coverage; write and send out press releases; and contact the local media. Set up a PayPal account or other facility to take advance payment as this is an important part of supper-club and pop-up ethos – to at least cover your costs.

Step 6: Book staff if they are needed

Give potential staff an outline of what will be expected of them and your plan for the evening – every person you speak to could bring in more customers, so sell your vision to them!

Step 7: Book to hire, buy or organise borrowing your supper club, pop-up restaurant or bar's dressings

Don't forget the small details such as candles, pictures, lamps and everything that will help create the right ambiance for your evening. Remember that the more you can get for free here, the greater your profit will be.

Step 8: Practise your menu

Once you're confident, have menus printed (up to this point you can tweak if it's not going according to plan). Order alcohol and glasses if needed; practise laying out your table; and check you have the correct number of everything for your customers.

Step 9: Get the venue ready

Clean and decorate your venue. Carry out your risk assessment on the area.

Step 10: Order/buy your ingredients and stock

Balance minimising wastage with buying the best quality you can. You're now ready for your first pop-up or supper club!

Working out your budget

OK, we're not going to teach you how to suck eggs here, but there are some basic concepts of budgeting that you need to factor into your plan if you want to come out on the right side of the profit margin. Use our simple budget tool below to help set pricing levels and tweak the vision for your pop-up or supper club plan.

Budget tool

Work out how long your pop-up or supper club is going to be running for – one night? One month? Make sure you work out the budget for all these costs based on the timeframe. You may find it's cheaper to run your pop-up for longer than just one night, as the set-up costs then become less when spread out over a longer period, with a fresh source of income from customers each days. Or you might want to cut your set-up costs right down, so that you can test the market with minimal investment.

Be as detailed as possible when working out your budget – you don't want to be hit with any hidden costs once you've got started that wipe out your profit.

Outgoing costs

- Rent of venue and/or business rates
- Staffing

- Utility bills
- Temporary Events Notice application
- Insurance
- Level 2 Food Safety & Hygiene course
- Hire of kitchen equipment
- Marketing costs – hire of photographer, copywriter, designer, social media expert, website designer or blogger
- Printing materials
- Cost of the restaurant dressings (tables, chairs, cutlery, crockery, lighting, props, candles, lightbulbs, napkins, toiletries and towel for bathroom)
- Cleaning materials
- Ingredients

The total of the above elements is what you need to make to break even over the entire period of your pop-up or supper club. This is the figure you need to take into account when choosing and pricing your menu, divided by the number of people you want to cater for.

Finding your price point

How many people do you need to cover the costs at your chosen price point? Look at your space, which will dictate how many customers you need, and consider all your outgoings and what would be a fair price for the kind of event you are planning. This will help you to pick the price point of your evening. And remember, it is unlikely you will fill 100 per cent of customer spaces every sitting if your pop-up is running regularly – make sure you factor in a margin for cancellations or unsold tickets.

Tweaking your budget

Review your budget plans – are there any ways you can save costs, such as utilising the skills of family and friends? Beg, steal or borrow equipment and look at what is really essential to your success. Could you run your own blog rather than paying to set up a website? There are always extra responsibilities that you can take on yourself, but you must weigh up the cost of your time against the cash saving – how much of a saving are you really getting? And ask yourself, can you carry out these tasks well, or will you be better off calling in the professionals? We both had a background in journalism, graphic design and photography, so marketing and PR was something we were confident of doing ourselves, but be honest with yourself, as a job done badly can ruin your reputation before you've even started.

Cost-cutting and raising capital

- Running your pop-up in a restaurant that already exists could massively help reduce your start-up costs.
- You could also team up with local suppliers who may allow you to use their cheese shop or brewery free of charge if you are promoting their produce as part of your night. And they will help with publicising your evening too!
- You may want to explore the possibility of getting funding from local authorities, trusts and foundations, or applying for grants. We have a list of these in Appendix 2.
- You might want to find an investor. Perhaps you have family and friends who would like to support your plans (and would rather their money was with you than in the bank).
- There are also various crowdfunding websites. This is a way of funding projects by raising money from a large number of independent investors, usually through the Internet. Here are a few of the best: www.fundingtree.co.uk, www.fundingcircle.com, www.crowdfunder.co.uk, www.crowdcube.com and www.seedrs.com.
- Finally, you could think about approaching already successful businesses or entrepreneurs with your idea and see

if they would be interested in investing, for a percentage of your profits. This has the added benefit of you gaining a mentor to help guide your through those first tricky months.

However, bear in mind that the minute you have an investor, you lay yourself open to losing some of your control and possibly creativity – the very things that will make your pop-up or supper club so exciting and unique. The pop-up ethos is all about creating something extraordinary on a shoestring – to be adaptable and quickly take advantage of untapped opportunities – so make sure any investors know that you need the freedom to realise your dreams.

CHAPTER 3
CHOOSING YOUR VENUE

The venue you choose is the stage for your evening. Get it right, and the wow factor is created for you before you lift a pot or pan. Get it wrong, and you'll have to work harder to get your guests on side.

Taking over an existing restaurant

Some already established restaurants will allow you to hold your pop-up night on their premises on a quiet night such as a Monday, Tuesday or Sunday, as you will bring in extra trade and help publicise their restaurant. They will usually offer you the space free of charge if you let them make money on the bar. This means you get access to a licensed premises, with all its health and safety and public liability legislation in place. They may even allow you access to their customer database to publicise the event. You will also be able to use the restaurant's table dressings and you could hire their staff for a night. If you're nervous about the legalities of a pop-up evening and don't want all the bother of paperwork, this could be the way to go, although it makes the event less unique to you and, of course, affects the amount of profit you can make.

CASE STUDY
TEAMING UP TO CUT THE COSTS

A group of MasterChef finalists took over an already existing restaurant in the Blue Fin Building in London for five weeks to host their own MasterChef pop-up in conjunction with Swiftsure Projects. Each week a different team of three chefs cooked their menu for 130 covers each sitting, catering for 12,000 people in total. It was the fastest-selling pop-up restaurant of all time and there are some fantastic lessons to be learnt. The venue was on the twelfth floor, providing wow-factor views across St Paul's and London's Square Mile, with a roof terrace for drinks. The kitchen was behind a temporary partition wall with windows set up between the diners and chefs, turning the whole experience into a kind of culinary theatre. Waiting staff encouraged guests to get up, wander around and take pictures. At the end of service the MasterChef finalists came out and mingled with diners, and chatted with them about their cooking, creating a truly interactive experience. Each chef only cooked two courses and the name of the chef was placed by their dish, so you made sure you got your meal from your 'favourite'. By taking over an already existing kitchen, the venue was fully kitted out, and by week five, the staff had got the service down to a T, meaning the chefs combined had a much greater chance of succeeding in their venture with minimised risk. Menus stuck to the perfect pop-up principles, including dishes that could be prepped in advance, such as pork and prosciutto terrine, and pistachio cake with burnt white chocolate ice cream. Sittings were staggered to ease pressure on the kitchen, and event company Swiftsure took care of the staffing and marketing. Yes, they may have had the MasterChef brand behind them, but by pooling their individual pulling power, it was possible to put on a much larger, more profitable event.

Using empty venues

Since the recession, there are empty venues all across the country, from businesses that went bust or a lack of tenants. These are currently sitting uninhabited and are costing their landlords an extra expense. A recent law passed now means that if a property is unoccupied for more than two months, a landlord must pay business rates – however there is a cunning loophole that allows landlords to get around this, which can be exploited by pop-up restaurateurs. If a landlord allows a pop-up business into their property for a month, the pop-up will be granted small business rates relief, and when the pop-up leaves, the landlord will be granted another two months' grace from business rates before they become liable again. Many pop-up restaurateurs are able to negotiate a peppercorn rent for a fantastic empty space because it is mutually beneficial to both them and the landlord. Look around your local area at interesting empty venues and think about what you could achieve – if a building has no kitchen this could be easily solved by hiring a temporary kitchen or setting up a barbecue.

Be inspired!

Some of the most amazing venues we've come across include a garden shed-cum-drinks laboratory called the Gin Shed, and a bespoke Alpine lodge created in central London serving fondues, hot cocktails and wild game.

How to find an outside venue

The best way to find the right venue for your pop-up restaurant is simply to get outside and pound the pavement. Take a notebook and pen with you, and walk through your local village, town or city, jotting down any empty buildings that might be viable for your pop-up. List the pros and cons of each space and make a note of any contact details for the landlord.

Don't be afraid of going off the beaten track and exploring down back streets and alleyways. And think of already occupied spaces that will be empty in the evening, such as coffee shops, which come with an already equipped bar space and seating area. Pop into other small businesses and ask if they know of anywhere that might be good locally. When you're back home, phone up the landlords and discuss your ideas – remember to point out the benefits in business rates relief.

Call your local council and ask if they know of any empty premises or community spaces which might be suitable for your pop-up restaurant project.

Search the web

There are also some great online resources to help you track down disused spaces that could be perfect for your pop-up restaurant:

- www.wearepopup.com – A one-stop shop for pop-up spaces across Europe.
- www.emptyshopsnetwork.co.uk – A site that aims to help people reduce, reuse and recycle empty shops and other spaces in towns and cities.
- www.popupspaceblog.com – A smart little blog with good legal advice for people thinking about entering the pop-up restaurant world.
- www.3space.org – 3space works with landlords to offer organisations that benefit the community temporary free-of-charge access to otherwise empty properties across the UK for pop-ups.
- www.40alfredplace.net/pop-up-restaurant – A space in Bristol available for hire for pop-up restaurants.
- www.meanwhile.org.uk – An organisation that uses property temporarily to help transform neighbourhoods.

Don't feel too cheeky about pitching to these unused spaces. Yes, you may get to use them for a peppercorn rent, but there are plenty of benefits to the owners too. After all, you may be about to spruce up their disused building, provide them relief on business rates and could potentially be bringing a new tenant their way – who knows who will be dining at your pop-up! Make sure you point out these benefits when you are pitching to take over the space, so they will be more open to your ideas.

TOP TIP
USE A FULLY EQUIPPED SPACE
Kitting out a restaurant is a big expense, and many up-and-coming restaurateurs choose to use existing kitchen spaces to hold their pop-up restaurant, with a cut going to the owners on the night.

Using your home

The ambiance you create for your pop-up restaurant or supper club is vitally important and gives your guests an idea of what to expect from the evening. If you are holding a supper club, it is likely to be in your home and you need to make sure you've considered some sensible elements such as:

- How many people can you realistically (and comfortably) fit in the space?
- Where are the toilets and are you happy to have strangers walk that route through your house to get to them?
- Can you move from the kitchen to your seating area carrying food with ease?
- How will your kitchen run on the night? Is it actually possible to cook your menu in your domestic kitchen for the number of diners attending?
- If you see any problems, adjust your plans accordingly: simplify the menu, reduce your numbers and get locks for certain rooms.

Some supper clubs still provide drinks by including a certain amount of free wine in the ticket price – it's up to you to decide what is appropriate for your event. You will also need to carry out a risk assessment on your venue and ensure your kitchen is up to scratch with all the health and safety requirements – it's rare that they come round to check but it's good to be able to show responsibility if they do. Speak to your local council and they will be happy to advise you.

CHAPTER 4

DEALING
WITH STAFF

Supper clubs tend to run on a fairly informal model, with a chef serving a group of people sitting around one table. They also tend to cater for a smaller number of people. This means you can save on the cost of professional staff, as you can bring food out already plated or rope in a friend or partner to help you with service. Pop-up restaurants are run on a larger, more professional scale and so staffing will be essential. This could range from a few well-trained family members and friends to actually employing professional staff on the night.

How many staff do you need?
Working out how many staff you will need for your pop-up restaurant depends on a variety of factors. You will need to consider:

* What kind of restaurant you will be running – for example, will it be fast food, fine dining or relaxed bistro?
* How you will be serving – for example, will people be queuing up at a street stall, treated to silver service, dining buffet style or eating a communal meal?
* What food will be on the menu – will you be able to prep and cook it all yourself or will you need assistance in the kitchen? Do you have enough crockery and cutlery for all your sittings or do you need a pot washer?
* The number of people you will be serving in your restaurant.
* How many useful family and friends you can rope in.
* Your budget for staffing.

TOP TIP
COVER ALL COSTS
Remember, if you are paying waiting staff you will need to factor this into your meal price and adjust it accordingly.

Run through the evening, think about every job that needs doing and see how much you can reasonably ask one person to do. Remember, people can multitask with small numbers of guests, but as the larger numbers come through the door, you will need to get your staff doing one job, over and over again, well.

CASE STUDY
IS IT WORTH THE INVESTMENT?
Factor in whether you're opening for a solid period of time, or occasional nights here and there. For example, the MasterChef finalists' pop-up restaurant in London took over the Blue Fin kitchen for five weeks so professional staff were required (see page 24), but if you're dotting dates here and there you're much more likely to be able to persuade friends/partners to pitch in around their day job.

Be inspired!

You could think about hiring in staff from a temping agency, or even approaching the local drama college to see if students would be willing to work on the night. Drama students are often great at dealing with people, are lively and outgoing, and if you are theming your evening they may well be game for getting into character!

> **TOP TIP**
> **BRING IN THE EXPERTS**
> Consider teaming up with a local wine company that has a member of staff who will act as a sommelier on the night. This means you can avoid the cost of paying someone else to do this, it provides you with a drinks licence and benefits the company as they get to showcase their products.

Your legal responsibilities as an employer

Also remember that if you are taking on staff, even in a part-time capacity, you will need to make yourself aware of the laws regarding their rights and responsibilities. Take a look at www.gov.uk/contract-types-and-employer-responsibilities/freelancers-consultants-and-contractors.

> **TOP TIP**
> **EMPLOYER RESPONSIBILITIES**
> Remember, even if your pop-up is running in a fairly informal capacity, you still need to make yourself aware of the responsibilities between an employer and an employee.

Using a restaurant's staff

If you are holding your pop-up in an already established restaurant, you may have the option of using their staff for the evening. This gives you the added advantage of an already trained workforce who are used to managing front of house and know how the kitchen and your venue works. This could really help with running your night – just remember their wages will eat into your profits, but you are sure to learn a lot from their experience, and their understanding of the dining room and kitchen.

TOP TIP
EXPERIENCE COUNTS
Remember, if you're using a restaurant's own staff they will be experienced in how the kitchen and service works, saving you time in training and paperwork.

Calling on family and friends

To cut costs, you might find asking friends and family to help you with running your night is a good idea. The benefits of this are that you already know their skill sets and are able to brief them on what you need them to do well in advance of the evening. Remember to be discerning about which friends or family you ask and play to their strengths. And roping in their help isn't just relevant for service and front of house – there are plenty of jobs that need doing beforehand, such as menu and poster designs, photography and fitting out your restaurant space, where you can pull in favours.

CASE STUDY
BE A JACK OF ALL TRADES
Remember, many people will be able to do more than one job. When we launched our pop-ups, Abigail was the social media whizz and front-of-house staff, while William was the poster designer, food photographer and chef. Between our abilities we could start blogging and tweeting to market our evenings. As we began to make money from our events we grew our budget for staff, but we still only ever hired the minimum we needed for each event. Any business needs to always think about how they can cut down the staffing requirements. Being only a core two-person operation, we took payment in advance and asked for people to

pre-order their menu. We left wine out on the tables, and ensured we had enough crockery and cutlery so that we didn't have to wash things up on the night. We kept the number of guests we seated down to twenty, so we didn't have to invest in extra seating and tables, and knew that was the number we could comfortably serve.

Briefing staff effectively

Make sure you give your staff a clear briefing of what you expect from them on the evening, before the night, including details of what you'd like them to wear. Formal black with a white shirt is a good default option, although don't be afraid to ask them to dress more creatively if it ties in with your theme.

Ideally, waiting staff should have tasted the dishes you're serving, so they can best advise customers if thay haven't ordered in advance.

On the evening ask staff to turn up at least two hours before your start time where possible so you can give them a recap, and they will be on hand to help out with any last-minute touches.

Explain the kind of atmosphere you're trying to create, so they can behave accordingly, and run through how you'd like them to deal with problems or complaining customers. A free drink is an obvious and simple way to placate any uncomfortable situations. Having an emergency bread basket on standby to fill in time in case of any disasters in the kitchen is an effective way of managing any backlog in service.

Being a good manager

Remember to delegate, however hard that may be when you're so passionate about your project. Explain to your staff they need to be your eyes and ears, and need to gauge the mood of the customers, communicating effectively with you and managing any front-of-house problems with a smile, so you can focus fully on cooking. Think about when you last had excellent service, explain to them why it was so good and ask them to replicate that – anything from the laid-back and welcoming approach of a gastro pub to the five-star, super-professional, formal service of the Ritz. Each restaurant has a different style of service and you need to emulate the right one for yours.

TOP TIP
LEADERSHIP MATTERS
As their manager they will look to you for leadership on the night – if this is not something you are confident doing, delegate this task to someone who is comfortable managing front of house.

Play to your strengths

Know your weaknesses and play to your strengths – know when other people can do things better than you and let them do it. No one likes a micromanager and it will quickly demoralise people from their role; by the end of the evening you will be running around like a headless chicken trying to do everyone's job for them. Empower your staff to make sensible, informed decisions. Unfortunately the nature of pop-up restaurants means you often need to take on waiting staff you've never worked with before and you won't know their strengths and weaknesses, so you need to be quick to pick up on when something isn't working. For example, you may find the girl you've tasked with welcoming people is in fact incredibly shy and you will quickly need to switch your staff around. Of course you can't be everywhere at once, so ask a friend to keep an eye on how smoothly everything is running and give you feedback on whether you need to step in or if something would simply work better running another way.

TOP TIP
TIPPING ETIQUETTE
Ensure that at the end of the evening any tips go to your waiting staff – without them the evening would not have been such a success and you will gain an enthusiastic bank of staff for future pop-up restaurant events.

CHAPTER 5

CHOOSING AND PRICING YOUR MENU

The menu is more of an art than a science. Yes, you'll need to make money, but your menu choices, including how you describe and price them, will create an impression relating to how your customers will perceive your food.

Finding inspiration

Let's not forget why you're doing this – you are passionate about food. So consider the evening you'd love to create with your artist's hat on, then look at that plan again with a business manager's head, and find a compromise.

When designing your menu for your first venture, simple is often better. Don't pick something with complicated timings (there is a great selection of simple, yet impressive recipes in Chapter 15) and practise, practise, PRACTISE your recipes before the night.

If you're struggling for inspiration, look at what's in season at the time of year you will be holding your event, and have a chat with your local greengrocer, butcher, fishmonger or game dealer about what they can get hold of for you. Not only will this help to shape your menu, but these items will often be cheaper at the right time of year.

A cohesive theme

The best pop-ups and supper clubs have a consistent theme that is well executed across the menu choice, service, ambiance and venue. So, if your dream is to host a celebration of Brazilian street food, it's not necessarily going to work with crystal glassware and waiting staff in black tie, with classical music playing in the background. Look at how your theme, menu and venue will work together. What props can you add? Our first supper club was in a Tudor country cottage, so to complement that we offered rustic game cooking served on wooden platters and charming farmhouse crockery; and we're currently planning a pop-up restaurant in a set of ramshackle oyster sheds on the Blackwater Estuary. We're using the local wildfowling club to row guests there and the menu will revolve around oysters, mussels, beer-battered fish, grilled mackerel and locally growing samphire foraged from along the coastline.

You also need to be realistic in what you will be able to deliver. Ask yourself what dishes you make time after time that get glowing reviews? If you're known for your fantastic Mexican cooking, don't decide to experiment with Italian on the night. A few pop-up restaurateurs we spoke to had cooked recipes for the first time on the evening, and all of them regretted it!

A journey of the senses

Think about the journey you want to take your diners on – it needs its peaks and troughs. Don't have three courses in a row of super spicy food, or two courses of chicken – you want to tantalise and stimulate the palate in different ways. Mix hot and cold, light and meaty, think about textures, sweet and sourness, tartness and richness. Remember, the starter is the appetiser, not the main event, so keep portion sizes moderate.

Think about whether the courses will clash with one another. If you're having a strong meaty main followed by a delicate dessert, you might want to consider serving a small shot glass of sorbet between the courses to cleanse the palate.

It's about time

You also need to consider your timings. Starters are often pâtés, salads and soups – all of which can be prepared in advance. Your main course is your chance to shine and usually requires more culinary skill. Puddings could be things that just need to be assembled by one of your waiting staff – cheeseboards, pavlovas, cheesecake or chocolate mousse, or if hot, cooked in large portions, such as locally grown blackberry and apple crumble.

Make sure you are confident in your menu, and this confidence will spill over to the customers, who will invariably enjoy their evening more.

How to price your menu

When picking a price point for the menu, most restaurants look at the cost of the ingredients they will be using on the night and multiply this by four. This should give you enough money to pay for your rent, staffing costs and bills. As much as this is your passion, you must remember that if you want to continue your pop-ups into the future, they are also a business. Look at existing restaurant menus and ask yourself why they have certain dishes on there and what price they are.

Find your target customer

Think about who your target customer is and what their disposable income is likely to be. Are your prices realistic? What are other restaurants and supper clubs in the area charging? Do your market research, visit a few and try to be comparable, but also ensure that you are not out of pocket.

Compile a spreadsheet with all your menu costs and cash flow, and make sure there's a profit there (see Chapter 2). This will also double up as a shopping list and will help with your pre-evening organisation. It's easy to fritter away an 'emergency bag of salad' here and 'a set of tealights' there, and discover you've got no profit left.

Remember, the only way you're going to make any real profit is cutting out the wastage, so ensure you only buy what you need, with a slight margin for error.

Making sure you get paid

If you are uncomfortable asking for cash face to face (as we were), it's easier to get people to pay before the night by popping a cheque in the post or setting up a PayPal account and means you will have cash flow for the ingredients. However, this also means you're less likely to get a tip on the night, but you don't have to keep an eye out for any of your guests doing a runner! If you're including, say half a bottle of wine per person, ask them to order in advance red or white, so, again, you are cutting down the costs of buying in the wrong type of wine to sell later.

If you do get people to pay on the evening, make sure you've planned when to ask them for cash and have some way of ticking off their payment – there's nothing more embarrassing than trying to charge someone twice!

Many people don't carry large quantities of cash these days. However, there are now several providers of great value, hassle-free chip and pin facilities available through PayPal and iZettle, which means you can take card payments on the night.

And whatever you do, if your pop-up is a sit-down affair, make sure people at least book in advance for your first evening – the last thing you need is extra people turning up when you haven't got enough food to feed them, or catering for an empty room.

CHAPTER 6
SELLING ALCOHOL

Some pop-up chefs would rather focus on the food and get a local wine merchant to organise the drink for the evening. This means the wine merchant would get the profit from the wine sales, but the restaurateur wouldn't have to lay out any money on the stock. It's also an impressive touch to have a wine expert on hand to educate guests on what they are drinking. Wine merchants will also be licensed, which will solve any issues if you don't want to apply for a Temporary Events Notice (or you haven't left yourself with enough time to do so). They will also probably have a database of customers, which you may be able to use to help publicise your event.

There are two things you need to know when deciding if you want to serve alcohol at your pop-up restaurant or supper club.

1. It's usually an area for easy profit at any restaurant.
2. Thanks to some lovely new legislation, the previously mentioned Temporary Events Notice (TEN), it's easy as pie to get permission.

Choosing your drinks menu

It may sound blindingly obvious but it needs to be said – having both red and white wine on offer is a must.

What you charge for drinks is up to you. In many restaurants, a £5 bottle of wine will be sold for £20, but the spirit of your pop-up will dictate whether your wine is more keenly priced or more highbrow than this. What you should do is put a little thought into it. Ask for a proper wine tasting at your local off-licence, tell them your budget, what you will be cooking on the night and use their expertise to get the best plonk possible. If you're theming your food from a particular region, see if you can try some wines that come from that area. You don't need to invest in a huge selection if you're trying to keep costs down. If you find something you like and it pairs well with the food, then one red and one white will be fine. You can, however, boost your profits if you stretch to a selection, as many people are naturally drawn to not select the cheapest wine on the list.

TOP TIP
TASTING NOTES
Ask the experts at your local wine merchant to help you write some tasting notes so you can share them with your guests on the evening – they will be impressed you've gone to such efforts.

CASE STUDY
FIND YOUR STORY
While travelling across Europe to import ham and bees, we stumbled across a fantastic small start-up, family-run single-vineyard winery in Spain when we took a wrong turning along a dirt track. We were invited back for a wine tasting the next day and ended up tasting the same, most fantastic voignier, for around three hours. We have now become the sole importer for this wine in the UK and their wines are what we sell at our pop-ups. Our customers love this story and it gives real provenance to the drink we serve.

And you don't have to just consider wine – there are plenty of other drinks out there for you to explore. Could your imaginatively named cocktail list add an extra layer to your story? We've held a Valentine's Day speakeasy with a moonshine bar, where the cocktails were so potent they should have come with a government health warning. We held it at a converted smugglers' pub called The Falcon and so, naturally, we took along one of our pet falcons to greet guests as they walked in the door.

The element of surprise

With pop-ups, the key is to think outside the box. Surprise, amaze and challenge everything people have previously expected about wining and dining. You could even turn the whole thing on its head and have the drinks dictating the food. How about a pie and real ale night, taking people on a seven-course tasting journey, pairing various pies with different beers? Single-estate ciders are now very popular and you could explore a tasting menu pairing some with flavours such as pork, venison and blackberry. The Wild Game Co and Scotch Malt Whisky Society collaborated on a pop-up where they paired twelve fine and rare whiskies with twelve delicious game tapas, with a guest speaker to talk attendees through the tasting.

TOP TIP
BEING EXTRAORDINARY
Rupert Ponsonby from food and drink PR specialists R&R Teamwork says: 'To get publicity you need to do the unexpected. You need a unique idea. We held an evening where every course was a different type of pork scratching and we paired it with different types of beer. For another evening we helped organise, there were over twenty different courses that featured haggis in some way! People were intrigued and came along to find out exactly how we'd make these menus work.'

Applying for a Temporary Events Notice (TEN)

If you're putting on a temporary event such as a pop-up or supper club and want to serve or sell alcohol (i.e. people will not bring their own and the drinks are not included in the price), you will need to complete a Temporary Events Notice (TEN). There are two types of TEN:

- A standard TEN, which is submitted to your local licensing authority no later than ten working days before the event to which it relates.
- A late TEN, which is submitted to the licensing authority not before the ninth working day and no later than five working days before the event to which it relates.

There are a few rules you will need to bear in mind, but most pop-up restaurants and supper clubs will easily qualify for this! These rules are:

- You need to keep the number of people at your event under 500.
- The event must last no more than 168 hours (that's seven days).
- The person applying can only apply for twelve temporary events per year, up to a total maximum of twenty-one days, unless they are a personal licensee.

Simple paperwork

You have to fill in an application form, which you can download from your local council's website, and pay a fee of £21. You send a copy of that form to the police and a copy to the Environmental Health, while the original is sent to your local licensing authority.

If you're granted your TEN, you will be able to sell alcohol to anyone over the age of eighteen.

You can find out more about applying for a TEN by contacting your local council, and we think it's really worth doing, as this is a fantastic way of boosting profit when running a pop-up restaurant or supper club.

Getting your Personal Licence

If you are intending to hold your events regularly as an actual business, you may want to think about getting your Personal Licence for selling alcohol, as this will allow you to apply for more TENs. If you have a Personal Licence, you can have fifty TENs a year, if you don't have a Personal Licence you can only have five TENs a year and each individual premises can only have a maximum of twelve. If you don't have a TEN and carry out an activity you should have a licence for you can be fined £20,000, sent to prison for six months, or both. So it's worth taking care of this paperwork! Make sure you display your TEN where it can be easily seen.

You can find out more about applying for your personal license by visiting www.gov.uk/alcohol-licensing.

TOP TIP
GLASSES AT THE READY
If you decide not to sell alcohol, and opt for BYOB, don't forget you will need to provide the glasses and have some wine chillers and ice buckets on standby for your guest to use.

CHAPTER 7
GET PUBLICITY

So you know you're a dab hand in the kitchen, are passionate about food and want to run a restaurant or supper club. But you need customers to ensure your evening is a success. You will need to think about how you're going to market your restaurant to get them through the door before you get busy in the kitchen. Luckily for you, pop-up restaurants and supper clubs have the novelty factor, which means people are curious when they hear one is going on in their neighbourhood. Add to this that it gives customers a chance to snoop round your home, or an interesting and unusual venue, and you've already got a handful of people ready to sign up! However, you can't just rely on this and there are some clever marketing tools you can use to make sure you're packed out every evening you're open.

Knowing your market

Where you publicise your event depends entirely on your market. We lived in a quaint fishing village, next to a busy pub on the high street, with plenty of passing traffic, and we knew our customers would not be coming from far and wide, but would be likely to be people we knew. We stuck up a poster and menu in our front window with our contact details three weeks before the event. Think about the timing of your advertising – too early and people will have forgotten about the event by the time it comes around – too late and people may be booked up. Try and create a sense of urgency and exclusivity so people are quick to book. The sooner you know how many are coming and what they're eating, the sooner you can get on with organising your night!

The power of the Internet

With pop-ups and supper clubs, more than any other business, it's vital that you learn to use the power of the Internet. You could start by setting up your own blog where you review local restaurants or post your own recipes, to build up a foodie following. We use WordPress and find it an incredibly simple and effective blog site, with a huge variety of ready-made, professional-looking templates, so even basic design skills won't be necessary. Visit www.wordpress.com for more details.

If you don't want to run your own blog, you can sign up to one of the many popular websites such as Find A Supper Club (www.supperclubfangroup.ning.com) to promote your evening. The way these websites work is that they will sell your tickets for you and add a small percentage to the cost of the ticket – usually 10 per cent. It won't affect your profit, and it makes it that bit more expensive for the diners, but it's a great way of connecting with food lovers in your area.

When deciding what your vision of your evening will be, try to think about providing something unique and unusual. Pop-up restaurateur cousins Ollie, Anna, Will and Ed launched Mile High to merge theatre with food for a whole gastronomic, role-play experience. But you don't need to do something as extreme as that. In our village there were also only a handful of restaurants, none of them specialised in game and people were intrigued that we'd shot it ourselves (provenance doesn't get much better than that!). Remember, you don't want to replicate what's already available – that won't interest people. So if there are nothing but Italian restaurants in your area, try to offer a different type of cuisine and emphasise that in your marketing.

Setting up a mailing list

We collected people's email addresses at farmers markets where William was selling his smoked meats and pies, and when we catered at outside events we would have a large glass bowl for people to leave their business cards in to take part in our 'lucky dips' to win a bottle of wine each month. Think of inventive ways you can encourage people to give you their contact details. This kind of information is invaluable, and companies pay big money to have access to this kind of material. If you've set up a Facebook page and Twitter account, could you hold a competition where people email you the answer to win an evening at your restaurant? With each of these ideas, you will need to make it clear that people's details will be kept for marketing purposes, just to make sure you stay on the right side of the law.

Using social media

Facebook and Twitter are also fantastic ways of publicising in their own right – set up accounts with the name of your supper club or restaurant. Think carefully about the title – it needs to be catchy, humorous and unique. For example, we're called The Shotgun Chef because we specialise in game, and our restaurants disappear as quickly as they popped up. Other great names we've come across that have piqued our interest include The Pig Club Pop-Up, which celebrated all things pork; The Mary Poppins Pop-Up restaurant experience where you're invited to dine with the infamous nanny and try your hand at being a chimney sweep; and The Surrealist Dinner Party, where an art installation is crossed with an experimental buffet, inspired by dishes such as Chevres hurlant de Tristesse (roughly translated as 'cheese of goat screaming in post-coital sadness'). You've got to make it a name that people will want to click through to and actually read about. The Rotting Fish would NOT be the kind of name to draw people in (although it would be perfect for a blog reviewing bad restaurants...).

> **TOP TIP**
> POSTING PHOTOS
> Make sure you take plenty of photographs of your delicious food in the
> run-up to the event, and post them on Facebook, Twitter and your blog,
> alongside details of your evening – food porn is one of the easiest things
> to get retweeted and shared online.

Get blogging

We set up a cookery blog called The Shotgun Chef (www.
theshotgunchef.co.uk) a few months before we held our first
restaurant, posting recipes, and updating people with news
about what we were growing in our garden, catching and
shooting for dinner, and our blog and Twitter accounts quickly
built up a following – we now have well over 7,000 followers,
and it's growing every day. We've found WordPress
(wordpress.com) is the most intuitive blogging site to use, but
there are plenty of other good ones out there, so just experiment
until you find one that you get on with. Remember to keep posts
to around 500 words as people have a short attention span
online and make sure your images are mouth-wateringly
delicious. If you're no good with a camera, invite a friend round
who is, and cook up a batch of recipes that you can write up and
post over the next month or so. If you're not comfortable writing
recipes, you could prepare a series of short articles about food,
such as what's in season when, or a series of profiles on small
local artisan producers – anything that will be interesting to
people who are interested in food, and will get them following
you on Twitter and 'liking' you on Facebook. That way, when
you do want to publicise your own event, you will have a ready-
made audience waiting there.

Short and sweet

With blog posts, once or twice a week is enough to keep people interested. Also check the spelling and readability of your post – don't forget that this will be many people's first impression of your restaurant and you want it to look as professional as possible. Make sure you share links to these blog posts on Facebook and Twitter too.

TOP TIP
MULTIPLE POSTINGS
If you don't have the time to regularly sit down and write a blog, you can upload several articles at once and timetable them to be posted in the future. You can use TweetDeck to do the same with your tweets.

Our village also had a lively online forum, so we posted details about our pop-up restaurant on there – check if where you live has one that is well used.

TOP TIP
EXPERTISE FOR LESS
If you don't have the time or don't understand social media, photography and design, there are ways of tracking down people talented in these areas without having to go through big-bucks businesses. Lots of business start-up networking evenings have small, independent graphic designers and copywriters there looking for work, at a fraction of a cost the big media agencies will charge you. Try Googling 'meetup' groups in your area or visit www.meetup.com and look under 'networking' and 'entrepreneur' groups, and you will find these are absolute hotbeds for the people you need.

The local press

Getting some publicity from the local and regional press is fairly easy, as they are always looking for content to fill their pages or airtime. But you have to help make it easy for them to give you coverage. We had a 'story' – we'd got engaged five days after meeting, because of William's fantastic cooking, and we eloped to Scotland two months later and got married on a grouse moor, where he cooked the wedding breakfast. We then started running pop-up restaurants in our cottage focused around the game we both loved to shoot and fish for. We'd got all the elements for a romantic and unusual story right there.

What's your angle?

So think about what your story is – have you dropped out of the rat race to follow your passion for food? Do you come from a long line of talented cooks? Is cooking what you've used as a kind of therapy to see you through the tough times in life? Ask yourself where your passion for cooking comes from and think, 'If I were a journalist interviewing me, what would be the juicy questions I'd need to ask myself to get the story out?'. If you're struggling with this, ask a close friend or family member what they think is your 'food story'.

Braving the critics

If you're feeling confident, you could invite a local restaurant critic to attend your opening night – although this takes guts and will put extra pressure on you in the kitchen, so you need to be confident the evening will go without a hitch (when they say there's no such thing as 'bad publicity', they are lying!). If this is too scary for your first event then ask them to come round beforehand and sample some of the dishes you will be cooking, and conduct a short interview. Believe us, as a journalist herself, Abigail can confirm they never say no to free food!

Be inspired!

Contributing to the community is also another angle to get you coverage in the press. Are there ways you can take on young people from a local catering college or offer training to students from a local sixth form college? You could even team up with a local charity to see if you could offer employment to out-of-work young people – all these things will encourage the community to get behind you, which is where your customers will come from. The local media will love this element and it will help with building 'your story'.

'Free' advertising

We're firm believers that you should never pay for advertising. Besides, that would go against the underground nature of the pop-up! The exception to this would be paying something like £5 to stick a poster in your local Post Office window, as it's targeted at, and supporting, the local community and so is relevant. If your concept is good enough then it will generate local press interest anyway. But don't think this means you can just sit back – you have to work to sell that story to the press. Ask yourself, what's interesting and unique about your pop-up? Remember, journalists' inboxes are flooded with press releases every day and are on tight deadlines – why should yours stand out?

How to write a press release

You're off to a winning start here, because you've already got the most important elements for a successful press release at your fingertips. You're doing something new and unusual, and everybody loves reading about food.

Write a killer headline

You need to come up with an absolute kickass headline in the email subject to grab their attention, such as 'Ex-clown launches pop-up fish restaurant in empty aquarium'. Don't try to be too clever or cryptic – it needs to be obvious what your press release is about.

Put your most exciting point first

Get your most important, exciting sentence in there first. Journalists typically write the opening sentence of a news story by answering the five 'Ws': who, what, where, why and when questions, so answer these for them right away. If they didn't read any further than that sentence, they'd have your story summed up! Abigail likes to throw in the 'how' here too, just for good measure. Try and summarise this in less than twenty words. Look at a news story in a *good* local newspaper and copy the structure of that.

Imagine you're in a pub

Another good tip is to imagine you are telling the story to a friend at the pub – how would you introduce it in an exciting and interesting way?

Cut it down

Keep it short and sweet. Don't write more than 400 words (the average length of a local news story). Put any extra, non-essential background information in a section entitled 'notes to editors' at the bottom. You want to stick to one sheet of A4 – no more.

Include a sexy quote

Ensure you include a couple of quotes from yourself, as you'd see in a real news story, which are pertinent and lively, and make sure they add something to the story – don't just repeat what you've already written. Use them to provide insight, rather than information. For example, how did your evening go? How were you feeling before it? What was the highlight of your menu?

How did customers react? Will you be holding one again? Rather than: 'Fifteen guests turned up and I served them potted crab and beef bourguignon'. Avoid dull facts.

Break it up

You can use subheadings and bullet points to make your information clear and legible, and this is likely to help you structure your press release while you write.

Make it targeted

Write your template press release, with everything you want to get across, and then tweak it for each publication you're sending it to. Change the order of facts accordingly and consider how they would report it.

Include contact details

Always include your contact details at the end and offer an interview (by telephone, email or face to face) to follow up the press release.

Check for mistakes

Finally, read through your press release several times and check for spelling mistakes and punctuation. If this is not your strong point, ask a friend or relative to help. This is important when projecting an air of professionalism, and could make the difference between a journalist pressing the delete button or picking up the phone.

Pick a contact

When you send out your press release, make sure you send it to an actual person, rather than just 'news desk', as it has a higher chance of being read and you can follow up your email a day later with a phone call. Have they received your press release? If not would they like you to send it again? Are there any more details that they need?

Picture perfect

Ensure you have lovely high-quality, high-resolution images of your food available on request for journalists. Upload these to an image-sharing website such as Dropbox or send them via a file-transfer service such as Hightail, as emailing these out can clog up a journalist's Inbox. If you can't take good pictures see if there's anyone talented in photography at your local sixth form college (their Art Department should be happy to help). Give them a credit and offer them a small amount of money – it will help them to build their CV.

Getting radio coverage

Think about what you could give to local radio. You could invite a presenter to your house and cook for them live on air or give one of their team a cookery lesson. Or how about sending them a sample of your food to taste on the breakfast show in exchange for giving your first night a plug?

TOP TIP
SELL YOURSELF

Even simple, old-school methods such as a poster outside your house or pop-up venue, or flyers through local letterboxes are still effective for publicity. The key to success is making sure people select their food and book in advance, so there are no nasty surprises on the night. A flyer with a menu on it will simplify the booking process enormously.

Designing posters and flyers

If you're making your posters and flyers yourself you will need to keep in mind some simple principles of good design to make sure these materials are effective. I'm talking about posters below, but the same rules will apply for flyers.

- Decide what the size of your poster is going to be.
- Work out how much information it's essential to include. If you want people to pre-order their menu you will have to make sure this is on there too.
- Be clear and succinct with the information you are trying to get across and use exciting language.
- Think about who your customers are and the impression you are trying to create of your pop-up with your poster, as this will dictate its style.
- If you are using images, logos or colours, do they all tie in with your overarching theme?
- Keep it very simple – if the poster gets too busy, the message will get lost.
- Keep your title short and to the point so as to grab the attention of the potential customer, make this the most important message on the poster, for example: 'New Year's Day Pop-Up Recovery Breakfast'.
- Ensure all the vital information is on there – especially your contact details.

Getting people talking

Word of mouth is a powerful tool. They say in marketing that consumers tell an average of nine people about a good experience, but twice as many about a bad one. This doesn't mean that it's an unmitigated disaster if something doesn't go according to plan on your night, but it's how you deal with it that counts. We're firm believers in turning bad PR into good

PR, and if you do miss the mark, give a sincere apology and offer diners something to compensate – be that a free glass (or bottle) of wine, an offer to put it right, a complimentary sorbet between courses or a slight discount on their meal. Use your judgement in the situation and ask yourself, 'How would I feel if I were the customer?' This helps dictate a measured (and human) response.

Creating a buzz

We would visit our local pub the evening after our pop-up and were always delighted the village was buzzing with stories they'd heard independently of our success. This gave us a chance to chat about our next pop-up to other people in the pub – essentially new customers. Likewise, we would blog about our supper club's success a few days after the event to let people know what they had missed out on!

> **TOP TIP**
> **CAPTURE THE MOMENT**
> Don't forget to take a few snaps on the night of your food all plated up and some customers happily tucking in to capture the spirit of your evening.

CHAPTER 8

RUNNING A POP-UP BAR

In wine there is wisdom, in beer there is freedom, in water there is bacteria.

Benjamin Franklin

You could turn the whole pop-up restaurant idea on its head and run a pop-up bar! Yes, there will be a large initial outlay to invest in drinks, but the profit margins are huge if you can draw in clientele. You could still add a culinary element by offering simple bar snacks which you can prep in advance – home-made antipasti, pâtés and artisan breads, a beautifully presented charcuterie, homemade pork pies, pickled quail's eggs – any good-quality produce to accompany the drinks you will serve on the night. Not needing access to a kitchen means that you're also able to take over more unusual spaces – think of empty railway arches, a barge, roof gardens, market stalls and beaches. Bars are incredibly mobile, meaning you can pop-up literally anywhere at any time.

Creating the wow factor

With a restaurant, it is the food that speaks for itself. With a bar, for customers, it is all about the experience you are providing from the moment they walk in the door. As you've already bought in your drinks, you can concentrate on the three keys to success – excellent drinks, fantastic decor and absolutely tip-top customer service.

With a bar, the little details are absolutely vital and your menu and drinks list is your first impression, especially if you intend to pin it outside a venue to tempt people in. Unless you have a background in these areas, have some professional photographs taken of the venue, bar snacks and cocktails, and ask a graphic designer and copywriter to work on your menu. Your menu is your 'advert' and if you do the hard work here, you're sure to get people through the door.

What's your theme?

Your bar's theme is paramount. The menu will give people an idea of what their experience will be when they step inside, so make sure it's cohesive with the atmosphere you want to create. Are you running a sophisticated wine bar? Then follow this through with an elegant font for your menus, softly lit photographs and bar snacks that complement your theme, such as pickled quail's eggs and asparagus spears. Your service would be discreet and the music playing as people arrive could be smooth jazz.

Are you running a brash, bright and buzzy cocktail bar? Then your menu should feature colourful images, with lively descriptions and bold fonts; the music as people enter could be a Cuban soundtrack and your bartenders' service could be cheeky. Just remember to make sure music is part of your TEN application.

TOP TIP
CHOOSING A THEME
If you're struggling to make your theme cohesive, try a trick that writers use when trying to form their characters. Imagine your ideal customer. Give them a name, imagine what they'd wear, the music they'd listen to, what their hobbies are, their job, and then imagine where they'd go for a drink or dinner – this should help you form an idea of their perfect evening in your mind.

Once you have designed your menus, post them through letterboxes locally and see if shops and hotels in the area would be happy to have a pile of them by the till or on reception – you could encourage them by offering to have some of their flyers in your bar, or offer the owner a free drink on the opening night.

Pricing your menu

Pricing is tricky, and again must be kept in line with the atmosphere you want to create and the kind of customer you are targeting. Price too low, and you will be out of pocket and will have devalued your bar brand in the eyes of high-end customers. Price too high and you're unlikely to get repeat customers or people staying for more than one drink, unless you're in a wealthy area.

Most bars work on the principle of multiplying the cost value of what they're selling by three for wine and four for beer, spirits and cocktails, in order to cover staffing and rent costs, and it's a good rule to follow. However, while this works well in theory, be mindful that when you've got a more expensive product such as a £6 craft beer, you may have difficulty in shifting it at £18! Be realistic about what people will pay, as goods sitting on your shelves for too long will be no good for anyone!

Finding your niche

Craft beers and single-estate ciders have become incredibly popular in recent years, so don't overlook the idea that people are happy to pay good prices for something other than wine. Likewise, the demise of the old-fashioned real ale pub, with nothing but a shove ha'penny board and cockles on offer alongside good-quality local beers, is something that you could look at reviving. As with a pop-up restaurant, your pop-up bar will need to be unusual, unique and offer something unexpected.

CASE STUDIES
NO HOLDS BARRED: THREE OF THE BEST

- The House of Wolf held a Day of the Dead Party in Islington on Halloween, complete with tequila, margaritas and a mariachi band. Guests were encouraged to wear full-on Mexican fancy dress.
- Fever-Tree hosted the Ultimate Gin & Tonic Pop-Up Bar, serving more than 160 different gins from a bar sprouting gin botanicals.
- Christabel's Botanical Bar offered a mobile pop-up venue serving botanical cocktails and British tapas. Customers chose between their spread of herbal syrups, local spirits and herbs from an inbuilt garden to create their own cocktails, suitably garnished with edible flowers.

TOP TIP
DRINKS PROMOTIONS

Think of all the tricks that are already used in the bar trade – a happy hour with two-for-one cocktails will help draw in customers and create a fun, buzzy atmosphere.

Getting experience

If you've never been behind a bar, your opening night is not the time to start! You need to get a taste of what to expect before your first night. Approach another bar or pub to get some understanding of what goes on and some basic training, or ask a local hotel or theatre if you could work behind their bar for free one evening if someone shows you the ropes. Keep your eyes and ears open and ask questions – remember, you can learn as much from a badly run bar as a well-run one, and this is your chance to watch others making mistakes so that you don't have to. If you are hiring in staff or calling on family and friends to help out on the night, you are going to need to show strong leadership and be confident in training them up. So get your hands dirty and be prepared to learn every job imaginable, from mixing mojitos to changing the till roll. If your staff have confidence in you, they will work that much harder.

What makes a good barman?

A good bar has staff that know the menu inside out. They can recommend a drink for whatever mood the customer is in and are fantastic people readers – knowing at a glance what kind of money someone will want to spend and how to pitch to them. Looking professional, presentable and knowledgeable, with quick and efficient service, is exactly what a customer wants in their bar staff – and remember no one wants to wait fifteen minutes for a drink.

Keep a lid on expenses

Make sure your drinks are measured correctly – this means customers can't argue about the size of their measure, staff will be able to keep to a consistent standard, and you won't be out of pocket. Keep a detailed inventory of what your bar is stocked with at the beginning of the evening and what is left at the end. This way you know what to order more of, and can see what is selling well and what is not. This will provide essential budgeting information and means you can keep a close eye on where any wastage is occurring.

If your pop-up bar is going to become a regular event, make sure you are clear with staff about what you expect from them. Let them know at the end of the evening if you're not happy about something in a calm and constructive way – being a good manager is tough, but leading by example and communicating clearly are two of the biggest factors that will influence your success.

Finding your customers

As with a pop-up restaurant, make sure you build up a mailing list and keep the themes of your pop-up bar fresh and exciting. After all, who said your bar had to keep the same theme each time you open? Changing your theme each time you 'pop-up' while using the same stock, tweaked slightly, could be the thing that keeps your bar the hottest destination in town. Listen to customer and staff feedback, and encourage people to come to you with inspiration and ideas – the best ideas can come from the strangest of places. And don't be afraid to have a little fun. We've been to pop-up bars where Pimm's has been served from tricycles, libraries where Champagne is served between bookshelves and a pudding bar, where plated desserts are paired with wine.

As with a pop-up restaurant or supper club, running a blog with appetising cocktail recipes, tips on food and wine pairings, and using Facebook and Twitter to publicise two-for-one offers, happy hours or gigs at your bar for local musicians is a smart (and cheap) way of drawing people in.

CHAPTER 9
DRESSING YOUR RESTAURANT

So, you've got your venue sorted, your menu planned, your publicity underway and now you need to dress your restaurant. Take into account everything, from the lighting, to the pictures on the wall, to the tables, cutlery and pepper pots. Ensure there is a cohesive theme right the way through all these items.

TOP TIP
SOMETHING TO REMEMBER

A menu designed beautifully in your theme and printed out on each table place helps to whet the appetite of diners and gives them a lovely memento to take away at the end of the evening. Don't forget to include details of your next event.

Lighting matters

Lighting is vitally important as it will have a big effect on the atmosphere. Harsh, bold industrial lighting will create a busy, buzzing atmosphere, especially if you accompany it with some upbeat music. Soft lighting, such as table lamps, up-lighters and candlelight, will create a more romantic, intimate feel. If using candles, don't forget to include these in your risk assesment (see Chapter 10). Experiment before the evening with different effects to see which creates the mood you're after, and ensure it complements the food. Authentic oriental Mandarin music will transport your diners to Thailand when eating your pad thai; accordion instrumentals will waft them to Paris in your French bistro; and an oompah band will add authenticity to your Bavarian beer and pretzel night.

What to invest in

The table and seating will also affect your diners' experience, and is often a tricky area for first-time pop-ups and supper clubs. Where are you going to get these from in large numbers? You could look into hiring some for the evening from companies such as PKL (www.popup-restaurants.com), which specialises in temporary kitchen and furniture hire for pop-up restaurants, and has a wealth of helpful advice on its website; or London-based Gorgeous gourmet (www.gorgeoushire.co.uk).

TOP TIP
HIRE IN FURNITURE
Approach local furniture shops in your area to loan you furniture in exchange for a mention on your menu – you may even send some custom their way.

Consider the space you have, and how you're going to seat people. Putting people on two or three long tables, all mixed up together, will maximise seating, but are the kind of people you're targeting going to mind being sat next to strangers? Remember most people come to dinner in couples so you need to make sure you convey through your marketing that it's a more lively, sociable night, and they might just end up mixing and moving around.

Our pop-ups comprised tables of four, as we had an abundance of bistro tables to hand, so couples would get to make new friends on an evening without losing that intimate dining experience. Luckily we've only ever had one couple who refused to sit at another table and share. Because we had staggered dining times and had turned our living room into a place where people could sit by our log burner and enjoy a glass of fizz while awaiting their table, this was something we could get around.

TOP TIP
BORROW LOCALLY

To cut costs you could borrow tables from friends, family or a local community group. If you're using tables from lots of different sources, ensure you've got matching tablecloths so that the look isn't too hotchpotch.

CASE STUDY
A PRICE TOO HIGH

Jimmy Garcia, owner of Jimmy's Pop-Up, says: 'For my first pop-up I borrowed all my tables and chairs from the local church and as payment gave them two free tickets. It kept our costs down, but oh boy did I regret that when I had to go to church at 8 a.m. the next morning to return them and join in the hymns with a blistering hangover!'

Consider how you are going to dress the table: pristine white lace? Plain mahogany wood, scattered with rose petals? Or the tables themselves could be the dressings – oak whisky barrels, old railway sleepers, tables and benches made of scaffolding – let your imagination run wild. Remember small details such as polishing your glasses and cutlery and ironing your napkins, and factor in the time you will need to do this on your prep day or get your staff in early to do this before your guests arrive.

TOP TIP
STOCKPILE RAMEKINS
Don't throw away the small china or glass ramekins that you get free with shop-bought desserts – these double up as fantastic condiment holders, butter dishes, salt and pepper pots and tealight holders which we found very useful on the night.

Don't forget to consider other areas, such as the lobby where people will hang their coats. You can even create the wow factor in the toilet, with a little attention to detail such as a beautiful potted orchid, grand Moroccan lanterns, vintage hand mirrors arranged in groups along the wall, a dramatic stag's head, elegant soap dispensers, and a luxurious hand towel and dressings in keeping with your theme. So, for example, if you're running a seafood evening, think of hanging driftwood carvings, placing a beautiful wooden boat in the window and using a scallop shell as a soap holder. Some lovely black and white photographs of the fishermen who provided your seafood, with a small caption below, will help establish the authenticity of your dishes.

Be inspired!

Be observant next time you go out for dinner. Notice the little touches that help give their place the wow factor. Don't copy them, but think about how you can transpose those kinds of details for your theme. For example, Mile High sends out a plane ticket to you before you 'FLY' with them – this helps to spark intrigue and sets the tone for the experience you're going to be entering into.

Transform their experience

Again, if you're holding a pop-up in someone else's restaurant, you won't have to worry about the infrastructure, such as tables, chairs and cutlery, but that doesn't mean you can't add your own unique touch. Could you dress the room with theatre props to transport your diners to a magical wonderland? Could you bring along a moveable grill and flambé some of the meal in the dining area, creating a sense of theatre? Could you create a 'dining in the dark' experience, where guests only concentrate on the quality of the food and are led to their seats in the pitch black, with only the waiting staff having infrared glasses?

CASE STUDY
COMING TO THEIR SENSES
Heston Blumenthal is a master of this kind of dining experience and is constantly thinking of ways to surprise and delight his guests. As diners eat a dish called Sound of the Sea, they nibble on smoked fish, edible 'sand' and 'seaweed' while listening to seagulls on an MP3 player. Nothing is beyond your capability, if you just let your imagination run wild.

CHAPTER 10

STAYING ON THE RIGHT SIDE OF THE LAW

There are a few important bits and pieces of legislation that you need to have in place if you're running a pop-up restaurant. These are less so if you are running a supper club, because of its informal nature, which means the lines are a bit more blurred between a dinner party with people chipping in, and a commercial venture. However, all of these pieces of legislation would certainly be an asset to you, and if you are intending to hold your supper club more regularly as a commercial venture, you would need to get these in place. Alongside your Temporary Events Notice, which you will need for selling alcohol (see Chapter 6), you will need to consider all the areas below to make sure your venture is legally sound.

Health and safety qualifications
The main causes of risk of health and safety issues in temporary catering are:

* Slips trips and falls
* Lifting, manual handling and upper limb injuries
* Contact with hot surfaces and harmful substances
* Cuts from knives
* Cross-contamination of food

These are basic areas of risk that common sense in the kitchen would try to avoid, but it's a good idea to take a final look around your pop-up or supper club before people arrive to ensure areas are clean and tidy. Have a mop and cleaning materials close to hand in case you do have a spillage, and a first aid kit for use in the unlikely event of an accident. Make sure staff know where these items are, and are briefed on how and when to use them. Also have a list of emergency numbers on hand to use if something does go wrong.

How to carry out risk assessment

Risk assessment is really important in protecting your staff and customers as well as staying out of trouble with the law – and it's quite simple to do. It helps you to focus on the areas that may cause harm and troubleshoot them before they occur (bonus!). In many cases it's something as simple as briefing staff to clear up spillages quickly, or making sure cupboard doors aren't left wide open for people to walk into – basic common sense really!

Of course, the law can't expect you to completely wipe out risk – let's face it, every day you walk down the street there's the possibility that something bad could happen – but you are expected to take measures to protect people as far as is reasonably possible.

Walk around your venue and make an assessment of what you think could cause harm to someone, and then decide how you could help minimise this. See our table opposite for an example of a risk assessment. Once you have done this, ask a friend or another member of staff to take a walk around and carry out the same assessment. See if you've overlooked anything. The steps you take could be as simple as getting your staff to warn customers of the steep stairs or pointing out a wonky floorboard as they come in.

CASE STUDY
RISKY BUSINESS

Here's an example of the risk assessment we carried out at our first supper club in our own home – as you can imagine, in a sixteenth-century wonky cottage, we had to make sure we took precautions!

RISK ASSESMENT FOR RUNNING POP-UP RESTAURANT AT THE OLD BAKERY

Potential hazard: Tripping over step as you come in the entrance.

Who is at risk? Guests and staff.

What is the risk? People could trip over and harm themselves.

Level of risk? Medium.

Risk-reduction steps: Keep area with step well lit; place a sign saying 'Mind the step', and point it out to customers as they are escorted to and from the dining area.

Potential hazard: Fire in the house.

Who is at risk: Guests, staff, neighbours.

What is the risk? People could panic, become trapped in building, sustain an injury from fire.

Level of risk: Low.

Risk-reduction steps: Have fire extinguisher in the kitchen; brief all staff on the two exits that will get people safely out on to the street; lodge Temporary Events Notice with the fire service prior to the event; clearly mark fire exits; brief staff on a safe meeting point so we would be able to check everyone is out and keep a head count of guests; ensure flammable stock is stored safely and that we remove rubbish from the premises each day; test fire alarm on the morning of event: store all candles in glass jars and tealight holders.

Potential hazard: Cross-contamination and food poisoning.

What is the risk: People become ill from the food not being prepared and cooked properly.

Level of risk: Low.

Risk-reduction steps: Take a basic course in food hygiene preparation; ensure the kitchen meets basic food and safety hygiene standards; prepare meat and fish separately from other food; take out personal liability insurance.

Identifying hazards

A hazard is anything that may cause harm, and the most important part of the risk assessment is how you would deal with it if it happened. Thinking this through clearly before the evening will mean you can fix problems quickly and efficiently if they arise on the night.

Once you've identified your risks, make a written copy, which will help protect you legally if anything does go wrong as it shows you took precautions. Also make sure anyone else helping you on that evening is made aware of the findings of the risk assessment – what the risks are and how they can be minimised.

Further info

There is plenty of guidance on the Health and Safety Executive's website (www.hse.gov.uk) regarding how to carry out a risk assessment for a small catering venture, with handy templates to help you through the process. You will need to look at the risks associated with catering and employing casual staff, and then make a note of the steps you are taking to minimise those risks. For fire risk guidelines visit www.gov.uk/workplace-fire-safety-your-responsibilities.

Security

You have a duty as a pop-up restaurateur or supper club host to take reasonable precautions to ensure people's security at your chosen venue.

If you are running a supper club, this involves not only the security for your guests' coats and bags, but also security for yourself when inviting strangers into your own home.

1. Make sure all front-of-house staff have a system for storing coats and bags somewhere secure – in a place where someone

can keep an eye on them. Also hang them in the order that people arrived so you know how to quickly find their items.
2. Make sure all areas that are closed to customers are clearly marked with a polite notice and, again, make sure you will be able to see if someone approaches these areas.
3. Keep windows and doors closed, and locked where possible, to discourage opportunistic thieves.

Register your event

Your local council will be much happier with you if you register your pop-up or supper club as a food business – it's free and can't be refused. Talk to them about what you're planning and they will tell you what they need from you – they're there to help rather than hinder. If you're finding there is a lack of cooperation here, find out what they want to provide catering-wise in the local area and see if you can offer what they're after as part of your pop-up. Building a good relationship with your local council will be key to helping your pop-up succeed.

Food hygiene

You should also have a Level 2 Food Safety & Hygiene certificate, which is simple to complete and you can easily do in a couple of hours online. Many different companies offer this, so simply type 'online Level 2 Food Safety & Hygiene course' into a search engine.

The Food Standards Agency's website (www.food.gov.uk) has some incredibly useful information on starting a food business (along with links through to the food hygiene courses), including information on how to contact your local authority, register your pop-up restaurant and a checklist for starting up.

Insurance

Public liability insurance

It is not a legal requirement to have public liability insurance for pop-up restaurants, but you would be mad not to, as it's not expensive and will protect you if anything goes wrong. The most obvious worries are things such as food poisoning, slips or falls, burns, claims from customers or damage to the venue you've taken over.

There are now insurance policies specifically for pop-up restaurants and supper clubs, which you will find online. Check your home insurance, as you may find that supper clubs held in your own home are covered by your home and contents insurance. Alternatively, you may find that your particular insurance policy will specifically not cover you for commercial activity in your own home. If this is the case you will need to take out further insurance. For pop-ups, an insurer will want to know when and where you will be popping up and how often you will be moving premises.

Employers' liability insurance

If you are employing staff, you are legally required to take out employers' liability insurance. It will cover you if one of your workers becomes ill, is injured, or is even killed while working for you. You are only exempt from this if you are using staff who are self-employed or if your 'staff' are volunteering friends and family.

One-stop shop

You may find that you can cover all of these insurance requirements in one pop-up policy, so be prepared to shop around and be honest with insurance brokers about what you're trying to do. It's their responsibility to find an insurance policy that fits you – not the other way around.

> **TOP TIP**
> TAX MATTERS
> You will need to pay tax on any profit you gain from holding your pop-up restaurant, so don't forget to factor this into your budgeting plan.

Business rates: the good news

In theory, you will also need to pay business rates on any non-domestic property you are using unless you qualify for small business rates relief – but for a pop-up restaurant it's almost impossible for you not to qualify!

CHAPTER 11
HOW TO RUN
YOUR EVENING

The 50–50–90 rule: anytime you have a 50–50 chance of getting something right, there's a 90 per cent probability you'll get it wrong.

Journalist Andy Rooney

The day before pop-up

This is your prep day. It's where, if you put in the hard work, the actual pop-up or supper club will run smoothly. We know from experience that our most stressful pop-ups were the ones where we didn't prioritise prepping the day before and ended up running out of time trying to get everything done.

- If you are hiring a venue it's a smart idea to gain access to it the day before so you can set up and make sure everything works, such as lights and kitchen equipment, that the toilets are clean and that all your furniture is set up as you'd like it.
- If you are renting cutlery and so on, have it delivered direct to the venue and check someone will be there to sign for it – the last thing you want to be doing is carting around extra furniture and kitchenware on the day of your pop-up.
- Check the kitchen is stocked with every utensil you need.
- If you are having food deliveries made, make sure your suppliers are bringing everything that can be brought in advance the day before, and if deliveries are being made on the day of the pop-up, call your suppliers to check everything is in order.

- If you are buying in fresh bread, fish and a few perishable items on the day, write these on a big notice and tick off items as they arrive.
- Tick off your shopping ingredients list with the menu next to you, going through every recipe step by step to make sure you have everything you need. Don't just think of the food, but remember the other touches, such as candles or fresh soap for the bathroom, ice for the wine buckets and fresh flowers for the tables.
- Get as much of your food prepped in advance as possible, such as sauces and marinades, and pluck and dress your meat.
- Make sure you have enough ingredients for a few extra portions of each course in case a disaster happens on the night.
- Imagine your diners' experience from start to finish and think of everything you need to make your night a success.
- Chill your white wine.
- Essentially you need to be ready to run your pop-up the day before your actual event.

TOP TIP
BE PREPARED
Remember to buy some blue catering plasters and a first aid kit in case you pick up any cuts or burns in the kitchen.

The day before a supper club

- See the advice on page 37 for preparing your menu for a pop-up.
- If you are holding the supper club in your own home, do you have room to set up the tables and chairs ahead of time?
- If so, lay the tables ready for tomorrow. If not, lay one place to check you've got everything you need, and count through

the items needed for the other places to ensure you have enough of everything.

- Check your cutlery and glasses are polished, your plates aren't chipped and your napkins are ironed.
- Fill up your salt and pepper pots.
- Check you have a corkscrew or two for opening wine, and make sure there will be enough room in the fridge to chill the white wine – if not you will need to pick up some ice and use this to chill the bottles in a bucket at least an hour before your guests arrive.
- What state is your kitchen in? Have you got enough space to prepare, cook and assemble your food? If not, make some!
- Is the part of the house that people will be using clean and tidy? If not, get busy! Don't just focus on where they will be dining, but also check the toilet facilities, the hallway and even the approach to your home. Are there bin bags strewn outside? Is there litter blowing through your garden? Look at your home as an outsider would – they are paying money for a culinary experience, so create a professional impression from the minute they approach your home.
- Check that what *you* are going to wear is ready – will you be in full chef's whites? All black? Remember to dress appropriately so that if your guests spot you it will create the right impression. If diners are paying on the night, do you have a float to give them change or card payment facilities? All these things should be organised ahead of the big day.

Prepping your staff

If you are having friends or staff to help out, give them a call to make sure they know the correct time to arrive (at least two hours before so they can help with any last-minute details and you can brief them properly). Also make sure they know what you'd like them to wear, and that anyone with long hair has it tied back.

TOP TIP
MAKE A LIST

The evening before your event, go to sleep with a pen and paper by your bed and if you think of anything you've missed, write it down to deal with in the morning – it's very helpful in getting a good night's sleep!

TOP TIP
TAKE A MOMENT TO VISUALISE

Visualise the evening from start to finish, with everything running perfectly. Imagine your guests arriving, how they will be greeted, watch them being seated, and see yourself cooking your meal in a calm, collected manner, with the dishes all going out perfectly and on time. See your diners happy and enjoying themselves. This visualisation technique is used by top athletes to help improve their performance.

On the day

In the morning

- Finish your prep, and complete and check the layout of the dining area.
- Check your camera is fully charged – you want to make sure you have some photos to capture your success and they will be very helpful when it comes to publicising your next event.
- Run through your menu from start to finish again – is there anything you've missed?
- Check all last-minute fresh items such as bread and so on have arrived.

Two hours before

- Get changed.
- Your staff should arrive. They need to be refreshed on what is expected from them, what you're trying to create and how you see the evening running, but this task can be delegated to someone you trust, so you can focus on cooking.
- One member of staff or a friend should be tasked with taking some photos of the food in the kitchen and of diners enjoying themselves.
- Run through the menu with waiters, so they will know how to describe it to guests, and answer their questions. Explain the wine choice to them and pin up some tasting notes so they can remind themselves throughout the night.
- Brief staff on how to handle guests who complain.
- Point out where coats should be stored and how to see guests out of the venue.
- Run through issues flagged through the risk assessment and also where the fire assembly points are.
- Explain to a competent member of staff how they can help with basic duties in the kitchen if things get pressured, such as plating up cheeseboards and desserts, just in case.

Open for business

- Your guests arrive. You should be in the kitchen, letting your front-of-house staff take over. Now it's time to cook!
- Once the cooking is over, take time to mingle with your guests over a glass of wine, chat with them about the food and bask in the glory.

CHAPTER 12
OTHER PEOPLE'S POP-UPS

Is there anyone so wise as to learn by the experience of others?

Voltaire

We spoke to a wide variety of supper club hosts and pop-up restaurateurs – from keen amateurs to the seasoned professionals – and interviewed restaurant critics to find out the secrets to their success. Here are some of the best stories we've heard along the way that could help make sure your supper club or pop-up restaurant or bar is deliciously disaster free.

The novice supper club

Freelance writer and mother of two Anna Blewett is a keen home cook and recently ran her first ever supper club at her home in Essex.

'I have to admit I was flying a bit blind when I held my first supper club, as I'd never been to one before. I'd noticed that pop-up restaurants and supper clubs had been gathering popularity on social media and, where as once upon a time they had been a super-trendy 'London' thing, they'd started to spread outside of the capital. After watching a few episodes of *Come Dine With Me*, I thought: "If they can do it, I'm sure I can too." I decided I'd theme my first supper club around British produce – not that adventurous, I know with hindsight, but for me, holding a supper club at my home was pretty adventurous!'

Making Money

'I had a clear idea it needed to be cheap if I wanted to make money, and I knew the key was to keep it simple if I didn't want to have to invest in loads of ingredients.

'I simply called it The Saturday Supper Club and advertised by putting flyers up around my local area. Social media was really helpful, as I discovered lots of local foodies on Twitter and asked them to retweet my event, which is where I think most of my customers came from. However, the disaster hit as soon as the first guest walked in the door. For the appetiser I'd ordered West Mersea oysters – a local delicacy where I live – and I'd intended to cook them under the grill. However, I'd never actually opened an oyster before, despite watching several cookery demonstrations, so I had to ask the first guest to help me shuck them. I tried to gloss over this by saying: 'I simply don't have the strength' – although I'm not entirely sure he believed me.

'My starter was gazpacho, as there was a glut of tomatoes in the supermarket in July – they were cheap, and tastier because they were in season. I knew I could prepare this in advance and, as it's served cold, it helped take some pressure off me in the kitchen; this course was thankfully a success. My main course was a warm beef salad served with rainbow chard, but the chard was tough and the water turned it a muddy colour as it cooked. Also, the butcher sold me topside of beef, which although I'd never cooked before, I took on his recommendation; I expect he hadn't advised me well on how to cook it though, as it was really tough.

Triumph at last

'My dessert was a triumph; pink gooseberry ice cream with elderflower jelly and homemade shortbread. I'd made a separate jelly for vegetarians and, thank goodness I did, because the gelatine one didn't set (I still don't understand why).

'I plated all the portions up, and I kept plenty of bread and pesto stocked up on the table, as I'd remembered Nigella saying you can create the illusion of abundance very easily with touches such as this. That was reflected in the feedback I got from guests, who all said they thought the meal was plentiful. I didn't sit with guests as I was so busy, but just came out at the end to check they had enjoyed their supper.

'The eight guests all sat down together around one table in my Victorian semi-detached, so I expect they felt more like friends than customers in my home. I charged £15 a head and everyone paid at the end of the evening, although that did feel a bit uncomfortable and you had to have some polite chat before the handover of cash.

'I organised the whole thing in a week – crazy, I know. One thing I did do well was to choose the ingredients that were expensive and that I wanted to promote, such as the oysters, and then found ways of cutting costs elsewhere to offset this. I also found a fantastic cheese, but it was pricey, so I simply served it in smaller quantities.'

Lessons learnt

'What I now know is that time matters and you never have enough! I'd overlooked just how key preparation is: washing wine glasses, lighting tealights – all these things can take so much time and I should have had this organised in advance. I had my sister and friends there to help but they were only really handing things round. I should have taken time to brief them properly well before everything kicked off. I have front-of-house experience so the service was important as far as I was concerned

– perhaps too important, as it distracted me from my cooking. In hindsight, I think I would have been more help out of the kitchen!

'I was massively ambitious but I did have really good fun, which might not be important to many people, but to me, really was. I had to feel excited and challenged by what I was doing, but I was holding my evening more as a hobbyist. If you want to charge proper money it needs to be right, so when I do it again I will spend time practising all the things I got wrong, so there are no glitches on the night.

'Another area that I'll look at for my next event will be the drinks. I held it as a BYOB because I didn't know what the situation was with licensing, and I also wanted to create an informal ambiance. Likewise, that's why I called it a supper club rather than a pop-up restaurant.

'After the evening I asked my diners for feedback and it was the tiny details I'd overlooked that had let me down – one of the things that was mentioned was about not having a hand towel in the bathroom. I realised I had to start looking at my home through a stranger's eyes, and imagine what their first impressions and requirements would be. One of the couples also said that before they came they looked me up online and were concerned I wouldn't be professional enough – I think I'd written a blog post somewhere that was informal and jokey, but this had put them off considering I was going to be cooking for them – so be mindful of the signals you send out. I was too casual about it all – what customers actually wanted to see was a professional, well-organised individual.'

The professional supper club

Luiz Hara is an Italian–Japanese Brazilian chef who has been running supper clubs from his home in London for two years, and runs food wine and travel blog The London Foodie (www.thelondonfoodie.co.uk).

'I set up my own food blog in 2009 while I was working in investment banking, and in 2011 I left my job in the City to travel to Tokyo and learn about cooking Japanese food for a year. I returned to London a year later to train at Le Cordon Bleu. I started running a supper club in my home as a way of practising what I was learning, as I didn't have time to work in a restaurant, but my events have become so successful that I now run them professionally. I got the idea for a Japanese supper club simply because nowhere else in London was cooking my food. I specialise in a cuisine called 'nikkei', which is Japanese food with a South American twist and it's the kind of food people will be eating in their own home in Japan rather than the kind of food you'd find in a restaurant.'

Conducting research

'Before I set up I'd been to many supper clubs and had done my homework, so I had an idea of how they ran and knew what I needed to do to make it successful.

'On my first evening I hosted it with a friend who supplied French wine, but now I simply run the evening as BYOB so that

I don't have to worry about licensing issues. As far as health and safety is concerned, each council has a different approach. For my own supper club, the council know I am a caterer and that I serve hot food within the premises, and they've been round to inspect my kitchen. Because I'm running my supper clubs as a business, I thought it wise to have insurance.

All hands on deck

'At the beginning, I did all the serving myself, but now that my events have grown to thirty covers I need to have help. All the staff muck in, from washing up, to hosting, to serving. For me the most important thing to ensure a successful night is a lot of planning. I spend the day before preparing the marinades and sauces and washing and chopping my herbs into Tupperware – everything I can do to be ready in advance.

'I think the key to making your supper club work is to bring in your personality and pick something niche. And have fun with it! My guests pay £45 for a tasting menu of ten dishes, and it encourages them to be adventurous. If they don't like something they know there will soon be something else for them to try.'

TOP TIP
DARE TO BE DIFFERENT
Don't be afraid to bring in your personality and make sure you pick something no one else is doing.

The novice pop-up

Dan Kenny runs The Set pop-up restaurant in Brighton, (www.thesetpopup.com) along with his two friends, chef Semone Bonner, and Ali Bell, who takes care of the bar. They run the evenings every couple of months on top of holding down day jobs.

'We started our pop-ups, as most good ideas come about, after knocking around some ideas in the pub. We felt the Brighton food scene was perhaps not really exciting and inventive enough, and wanted to provide a different kind of experience to what was already being done. Our mission statement was food in unexpected places, and foods that weren't necessarily available locally either – we'd all done a lot of travelling and wanted to bring that to the table. It had to be good fun, with a truly interactive experience for diners, often cooking in front of the customer at the table.'

Consider practicalities

'Before we started, every available day off I'd be walking around Brighton, looking for a venue. On our checklist was a place that wasn't too well known so wasn't too expensive, and more importantly, had the facilities which meant we could pull off the evening. Some places we saw were visually fantastic but the evening would have ended up a bit style over substance – you need the basics such as gas, electricity and toilets (yes, I'm not joking – think about these things!). And we knew we wanted customers to see us cooking, so we had to bear that in mind as well. Our rule is to never do the same venue twice as we want to keep customers guessing.

'For our first pop-up we hired a coffee bar, but didn't have a proper kitchen so we used lots of props instead, such as dehydrators, cream canisters and smoke guns, so that we could create a spectacle in front of our diners. Using the coffee shop bar, we created a platform, using the long surface top for our display. We still always make sure we create at least one plate of every dish in front of people for every pop-up. One of our first ideas was to make "dropped ice cream", where we place acetate sheets (which are see-through), on the table and literally build a tower of dessert in front of the guests so it looks like we are plonking the ice cream directly on the table!

'I think part of the key to our success is that we are different to what else is happening on the food scene in Brighton – we don't take ourselves too seriously.'

Collaborate with others

'Interestingly we did a collaboration with an Indian restaurant, as I'd spent some time travelling around Asia, and I loved those foods and flavours.

'We've been holding pop-ups every couple of months but we take a break when it gets busy in our day jobs. However, we've got three or four planned for 2015 and, interestingly, we've got venues around town which are approaching us now to put on a night – they've seen us online and pictures of our food being retweeted, and want to be involved.

'We invested a little of our own money, and all the profit we've made after costs we've reinvested, be that for fun cooking equipment, props or whatever.

'Of course, the dream is to have our own restaurant, but it's early days and the pop-up model works well with our current jobs.'

Challenges along the way

'There are a few things I've learnt along the way. For our first event we couldn't get into the venue until 2 p.m. on the day, leaving ourselves a lot of prep to do in three hours – it was stressful to say the least. Now we make sure we have the kitchen hired out the day before, so if anything does go wrong we always have plenty of time to rectify it.

'One of our secrets is that we constantly make lists, which are a great way of staying organised between the three of us – they mean we don't leave anything to chance.

'What was very helpful when we were starting up was that my sister works in marketing and she's been great – if there's one thing I'd stress, it's call on the skills of family and friends.

'One of the hardest things we found when we first started was selling our tickets through Twitter and Facebook and having an online presence. It took a long time to get those pages up to a standard where people would take us seriously. I'd go to work – on chefs' hours – and come home and work on our blog and social media. But now it's got momentum, so it's a little bit less effort! The "dropped ice cream" stunt got us about 100 new Twitter followers so think about what you can do visually to create a bit of a buzz.

'We get people asking to work for us which is really nice and when we're out and about and come across great service, then we poach those staff! Our staff are all self-employed, which means there are no legal responsibilities as an employer, and that makes sense when our pop-ups are so far apart timewise.'

A work in progress

'We serve seven courses of food and two courses of drinks for around £60, and we're still working out the perfect cover size. At our first pop-up we turned twenty-five tables in two sittings, so that's a total of fifty customers, which is hard work for staff. At the next one we did one sitting of thirty-eight and this worked better for us.

'If you're thinking of starting a pop-up or supper club – go for it. Make sure you have good people around who you can trust and are hardworking, and make sure you're well prepped, even down to the little details.

'But the most important thing is to go into each one with a smile on your face, brimming with an enthusiasm and a passion for what you do – after all, that's the essence of what makes a pop-up restaurant and will see you through!'

TOP TIP
AN EXTRA DAY
Try to hire out the kitchen the day before so you can get yourself acquainted with the equipment and layout – no two ovens are the same!

The professional pop-up

Ed Templeton is one of four cousins who launched Shuttlecock Inc. (www.shuttlecock-inc.com), a 'dining experiences' company that fuses great food with theatre and cinema. One of their regular themed pop-ups is Mile High, based on *Mad Men*-style dining, where guests are 'transported' to a different location on their 1950s 'aeroplane' set, tasting the cuisine of that destination.

'The idea was to combine amazing food cooked by chefs who work in the best London restaurants, and to merge that with theatre, using actors who we found at drama school to create a totally unique dining experience. People walk in off the street with no idea what to expect of the evening: it's about who they meet, our venue's decor dressed in fantastic props and bringing the set to life around them. But we never forget that food is at the heart of it all.

'Oli, my younger brother, is the chef and we run the evening with our two cousins. We've all grown up together having big, joyous family meals, and food has been ingrained in us all as the idea of people coming together to have a good time.'

A solid background

'The four of us were all already plugged into what was going on in the food scene in London, and then a couple of years ago we got talking – wouldn't it be fun to literally transport people to a new place? – and Mile High was born. We left our various City jobs in areas such as media and advertising. Our secret weapon was Oli, who had been working as a chef at London restaurant Moro.

'The supper club movement is all about the food and being in an intimate environment. Pop-ups take it to a larger scale and our events are all about creating something extraordinary out of the ordinary. We expanded into other events, such as Rumble at the Deli – where two talented young London chefs go head-to-head for three rounds of no-holds-barred culinary one-upmanship. The winner soaks up the applause, the loser washes up the pots and pans. We love the pop-up model because if things carry on for too long, the novelty of an event such as this can wear off. But if you hold them in short bursts, there's a real enthusiasm – we create the atmosphere of "it's a big party and everyone's invited!".'

Vertical take off!

'Our learning curve was pretty steep. The first Mile High destination was Gothenburg, serving up food such as chargrilled elk with golden beetroot through a glamorous fantasy inflight experience, and we held it while all of us were still in our previous jobs. Because we knew from the beginning that we wanted to make this our full-time job, we were very focused on making this a success and really ramped up our efforts a couple of months before. We invested money in dressing the place – tables, cutlery and so on, although you could hire that all if you were only doing it as a short-term venture. Being related gave the four of us the confidence to step into the unknown.

'After the first successful Mile High event, our events company Shuttlecock Inc. sprung from that. We built a kitchen in what was an old sorting office. We had to fine-tune a nigh-on-impossible task and I would advise people to know their limitations – understand what you can and can't deliver. Then execute your evening well.'

Selling alcohol made easy

'Organising the licensing to sell alcohol for our events was one of the pleasant surprises. We simply applied for a Temporary Events Notice, which allowed us to sell booze to anything between ten and 500 people. We've been to pop-ups where you get a drink included in the ticket to avoid the red tape around selling booze, but a lot of your profit comes from having a licence, so do consider a Temporary Events Notice if you want to maximise your profit.

'We've learnt a few lessons along the way – for example, we've had live music at some events and you need extra permission for that. Our chef Oli already had his food hygiene certificate from his previous time working as a chef, but nobody came to inspect our kitchen – we just looked at the legal requirements and made sure they were followed in case anyone ever did.

'When we started our pop-ups, suppliers scratched their heads a little as they had never been asked to do deliveries to different locations every few weeks. Since the credit crunch there are these empty buildings all over London, and our council has a lot of goodwill towards us using these spaces for a few weeks – it helps to regenerate the area. My advice would be to be mindful of what councils want to hear. Check out their websites and carry out a risk assessment, think about fire safety and if you will be a public nuisance. If you can, say 'I've got it covered' then they will be much more interested in helping you.'

Don't be fooled

'I've been to a few pop-ups and I think sometimes there can be the feeling that because anyone can, in theory, hold one, there is an assumption that it's OK for things to be a bit rough around the edges. But for us, pop-ups are about blowing people's minds. Leave them with a memorable experience – where they walk away thinking: 'I can't believe that just happened!' But never forget the food's got to be great. We charge £65 for Mile High, with four courses, but there is a lot of drink included in that, as that's a big part of the atmosphere of our night, so decide what's important for yours and give that special attention.

'The model we have of selling tickets up front means there's no wastage in the kitchen and staffing-wise you're all set up as you know how many are coming.

'Finally, you can't underestimate the power of social media. Try and get someone you know who is a bit media savvy to give you some advice as it will pay back tenfold.

If you're thinking of running a pop-up restaurant, just do it! It's not impossible! There's a lot of hard work involved, and your first event can be quite scary, but DO take that leap of faith and be confident in your food. We've had evenings that are not lucrative, but by the next event, you've learnt from it and you make that a success.'

TOP TIP
HANDLING THE COUNCIL
Be mindful of what councils want to hear. Check out their websites and carry out a risk assessment. Think about fire safety and if you will be a public nuisance. If you can say 'I've got it covered' then they will be much more interested in helping you.

The Pop-Up King

Jimmy Garcia has been labelled 'the Pop-Up King'. He's held dining experiences in locations from rooftops to tepee wedding camps and will even transform anyone's home into a pop-up restaurant for the night (www.jimmyspopup.com).

'I started learning how to chef while still at school and did a ski season working as a chef in a chalet. I then went to university to do business economics, and in the summer holidays got a job on a yacht as a private chef. When I graduated I started working in the City and hated it, so began running supper clubs in my own home and it all exploded from there. To be honest I would never have imagined it would be so popular so quickly.

'On my first night I was crapping myself, as hosting a supper club is different from simply cooking for people. To be honest, I really doubted whether anyone would want to come to my house and eat. The staffing was sparse – it was just me in the kitchen, and two of my friends were waiting staff, but I can tell you, further down the line, when you start to get popular, don't scrimp on the staff as they help keep everything together.'

The perfect combination

'The exciting thing about pop-ups is the timing – we were doing the right thing at the right time, which was partly the secret of our success. But remember, pop-ups are about putting yourself out there, putting yourself out of your comfort zone. It's difficult to explain what makes one pop-up or supper club so much better than another because it's about that chemistry that makes the right atmosphere. It's the venue, the food and the people, and you can't neglect one of them. Whether that's going to someone's home to have an intriguing look around or an unusual outside location where you are completely immersed in a totally unique environment.

'The most important advice I would give to anyone doing their first pop-up is don't run before you can walk – start simple. With your menu, for your first one, I'd advise a dish you can finish off in the oven. If it's undercooked, you can always put it back in, but if it's overcooked, you're fucked! Also slow-roasted dishes are a good bet – this makes it sound and look like you've spent a lot of time but, in reality, makes your life easier in the kitchen.

'When you're starting out, don't always expect the next one will sell out. For the first few pop-ups I held I was begging people to come and it takes a while to build a following, so you can't allow for mistakes. If you get it wrong, people will not want to pay. I went to a pop-up and paid £35 for a beef cheek I could have thrown at the wall – and I'm not the complaining type! If you're doing it to make a quick buck and not for a love (and talent) for cooking, it's pointless.'

TOP TIP
START SIMPLE
Don't run before you can walk – start with easier dishes as it takes a while to build a following, so you can't allow for mistakes.

The pop-up collaborators

Rupert Ponsonby and Emanuele Barasso run R&R Teamwork (www.randr.co.uk), which specialises in food and drink PR. They regularly collaborate with pop-up chefs to build a buzz around their products.

Rupert says: 'Beer is my real passion so we set up a beer school in 2003 to train up beer sommeliers to actually teach beer tasting to a truly professional level. We now have fifty beer sommeliers that we supply all over the world, and we work with different chefs who already hold their own supper clubs and pop-ups and introduce them to our drinks. To get some real attention, we needed to do things that the wine boys weren't doing, so we started to pair our beers with unusual foods – things such as smoked fish and smoked meats, sushi, cheese, chocolate, puddings. We even held a beer and oyster dinner and a seven-course pork scratching tasting menu, which included a fish pie with a pork scratching crust (absolutely delicious). We work with different chefs who showcase our ingredients, and it's a great idea! If you're a great local food producer, get together with a chef and hold a pop-up to showcase your product, with your food being used in unusual and exciting ways. Think outside the box! We worked with James Ramsden recently on a haggis-promotion menu, and even ended up with haggis soup!'

TOP TIP
LOCAL TIES

If you live in an area that is well known for a particular type of food, such as seafood, salamis or cheese, approach local producers and see if they will give you a deal on the food if you host an evening showcasing their ingredients. This will give you your theme and help build important ties with local suppliers.

The pop-up critic

Victoria Stewart, food editor of the *Evening Standard*, has been to every London pop-up restaurant worth knowing about, has a wealth of experience regarding what makes an event a lip-smacking success and runs street food blog London Street Foodie (www.londonstreetfoodie.co.uk).

'I got involved with London's pop-up food scene through working on the paper and having to try new things. Living in London is exciting and creative, and what I loved about the scene was that I would go to events and be introduced to a new chef or new experience of food. In the past three or four years there's been a massive resurgence in London food, it's become much more exciting, and pop-up restaurants and supper clubs have been a massive part of that.

'For a pop-up restaurant to "work", it's important to remember that you mustn't make the theme too cheesy. Be authentic, without going over the top. So, for example, if you're cooking Spanish, remember you're serving this, not in Spain, but in the UK, so you will never replicate that food completely. Instead, give your evening a slightly different twist. A set tasting menu is a great idea, meaning you can make sure things work such as the seating, front of house, and all the other details. It's always good to have entertainment, but again, make sure this is actually good, and not too much in the diners' faces.'

A warm welcome

'One thing I would always say is that it's good to have a welcome drink as people arrive – in the City, a lot of people are coming to you straight from work and are fairly stressed. Others may never have been to a pop-up or supper club before and may be a little apprehensive, but all of them will need something to ease them into the experience, and a welcome drink helps them relax.

'There's such a wide variety of pop-ups that I've been to – from big drinks brands that want to put on a grand experience to promote their products and throw you into a random space, to two chefs collaborating under one roof in a restaurant – that's always exciting as you never know what's going to happen.

'The thing that makes a pop-up restaurant different from a permanent restaurant is the idea that you may "discover" a new up-and-coming chef when you go there; you will never have stumbled across them anywhere else. Also it feeds into the excitement of the evening that it's temporary and you might miss out on something – it's a transient, once-in-a-lifetime experience. I also think it's a much more fun experience – it make a great first date, as pop-ups and supper clubs are usually very sociable; with a restaurant you go with the people you know and you talk to them all night and you follow that ritual. With pop-ups you're forced to interact and there's a lot more to talk about generally, as the whole evening is a sort of experiment – you won't just remember the food, you will remember all the small, creative details.'

High expectations

'I've had a few bad experiences. I went to a pop-up recently, and it was a very reasonably priced £25 for three courses – I'd enjoyed eating the food from their street van previously, but on the night, nothing turned up for at least an hour and the service was utterly slapdash. When I complained, their response was 'What do you expect for £25?', but the point is, if you're marketing yourself as a 'restaurant' then that's what you have to deliver. As I said before, it's not just about the food. Most of the good pop-up restaurants in London sit at around the £55 to £65 price mark, and you get a lot for your money – good food, interesting venue, great entertainment – so people's expectations are high.

'Make sure you test key things before the big night – can you cook the menu competently? Have you got a well-executed plan with the sittings? One of the best pop-ups I've been to is Burger Monday, which gets different celebrity chefs to cook a different signature burger each night. Host Daniel Young holds two or three sittings an event, and sits sixteen people at a time; the food is on time and cooked to perfection. It's a simple concept and it's been running on and off for a few years, but every night is different, and it sells out in literally minutes on Twitter.'

Know your market

'My advice for anyone thinking of holding a pop-up restaurant or supper club for the first time is don't just launch into it – they take a lot of planning. Make sure you see what is out there on the market – get to know what the standard is that you're competing with, visit or read up on other pop-ups and get a clear idea of what you're trying to do.

'Also check your price point is competitive, but remember to weigh up the cost of providing a good experience as opposed to something that's cheap, but not too cheerful. Consider what you think it's important to include. Yes, people do make the career leap into running pop-ups full time, but a lot of them already have experience running events companies or working in hospitality and catering, so make sure you pick up those skills before you change careers full time.'

TOP TIP
GET COMPETITIVE
Check your price point is competitive, but remember to weigh up the cost of providing a good experience as opposed to something that's cheap, but not too cheerful.

CHAPTER 13

WHAT TO DO IF THINGS GO WRONG

Invariably, things will go wrong during your time as a pop-up restaurateur or supper club host – especially if you plan to hold them as regular events. A smile and an apology go a long way, but you have to learn to read people quickly, and if you're not out on the floor, your staff need to be your eyes and ears, and respond to situations swiftly and discreetly. An annoyed customer can disrupt everyone else's experience.

Five pop-up mishaps – and how to cope

Here are some common pop-up problems and suggested ways to deal with them – although every customer is different and you will have to trust your own judgement!

You've run out of time for prepping

However tempting it is to call everyone into the kitchen to help, it's vital you let front of house continue to look after the customers. Take a deep breath and get one person to organise emergency bread baskets. If it's really going to be a long time, someone else can go round, offer everyone a free drink and apologise that the chef is a little behind schedule. A small amount of generosity can get most people on side.

You've dropped crockery

Make sure you have a few extra emergency glasses and crockery as accidents often happen in the flurry of service. If you still haven't got enough, get somebody to wash up from an earlier service, or think how you can adapt a later dish to be a sharing platter between two people – we've served the cheeseboard and puddings on a slate, and puddings in vintage teacups in just this situation.

The meal is burnt

Assess the situation – is it salvageable at all? Are there ways you can reduce the portion sizes of each serving to make it stretch? As a precaution you should always have extra ingredients for each dish you are cooking and don't forget the kitchen timer is your best friend to keep you focused under the pressure of service. If it's beyond salvation, apologise to the customer, and offer them a different dish and something complimentary as compensation.

Drunk customers

If a customer is causing disruption by being too drunk in your pop-up, stop serving them alcohol immediately and offer them water and coffee. Make sure someone calls them a taxi to get them home safely. As tempting as it is to want to get rid of them quickly, under no circumstances allow them to drive home.

A Twitter rant

If a customer has taken to Twitter to bad-mouth your evening, ask them to contact you privately. There is something about posting online that makes people capable of unleashing a torrent of hatred and criticism that they'd never say to your face. If the criticism is constructive then this can be helpful for your next pop-up, but if it's unreasonable and antagonistic, leave well alone.

REMEMBER

- Pay respect to the customer
- Fix the problem
- Offer compensation
- Don't respond to negativity unless dealing with it face to face

How to turn it around

Overwriting with new memories

If you have really messed up one dish, don't get flustered, but overwrite that bad memory by outperforming on the next course, or at your next event. People remember their most recent experience most vividly, so don't give up and vow to do better next time.

A sincere apology

If you really can't rectify something that has gone wrong, a sincere apology when you've got time to escape from the kitchen will mean a lot to a customer. Communicate with them quickly (whether it's through the staff or face to face) about what you have done to put the problem right.

Turning bad PR into good PR

Try to see a disaster as an opportunity to turn someone into a loyal customer. Fixing their problem can actually turn into a positive experience, and make them feel special and looked after.

Even seasoned pop-up hosts face challenges

Read reviews, take any criticism on the chin and try to find something in it you can learn from. Remember you can't please all people all of the time, but you will often please some. Listen to articulate, justified complaints and vow to fix those next time.

Remember that adage: 'The customer is always right' – even when they're wrong.

CASE STUDY
EVEN SEASONED POP-UP HOSTS FACE CHALLENGES

Ed Templeton of Mile High says: 'At one event, we had some power-hungry equipment that blew the mains power so we had to ditch the dishwasher and start handwashing dishes between the courses.

'We also had a charcoal grill in a small room, and ended up having to waft smoke out of an open window. We've also experienced deliveries not coming on time, or couples who came together who were teetotal, and, unfortunately for them, Mile High is a big party – people are encouraged to eat, drink and be merry. They complained and usually we'd hand out a free bottle of prosecco, but obviously this didn't work here! Our way around it was to apologise and invite them to our next event with complimentary tickets. If people complain, you have to take what they say on board and don't make them feel out of hand, as their opinion is valid and you can always learn something from what every customer says, even if you don't like to hear it!'

CHAPTER 14

BUILD ON
YOUR SUCCESS

Now, you've held your first, fabulously successful pop-up event, but where do you take it from here? Don't lose momentum!

Learning lessons
Making an appraisal after each event and being honest with yourself about what you could have done better, and indeed what you want to build on, is the key to every successful business.

- Look back on your evening: what went right, and what went wrong?
- How could you prevent those mistakes from happening again and how could you grow the good parts?
- One of the keys to being successful at anything is to know your strengths and your weaknesses, and to focus on your positives and get help with your negatives.
- Do you need assistance from other people in certain areas?
- Should you change your suppliers?
- Do you need to go for an easier menu?
- Do you need to get an alarm to help with your timings?
- Would you benefit from practising certain culinary skills?
- Do you need to simplify the payment process?
- Do staff need better training?

Publicising your success
Get in touch with the local paper and radio station, and tell them about how fantastic your evening was. Ask them if they'd

like to do a story on you, or come and do a restaurant review at your next event. Offer to write a regular recipe column for free in the paper in exchange for including details of your next pop-up event – these are all ways you can get free advertising without paying a penny, and all they require is a little bit of effort from you.

Blog it

Hopefully you found time to take some fantastic pictures of your food and the people attending, so use these to blog about your evening and publicise the next one.

Write about your event, emphasising what went right (rather than wrong) and make sure you get your personality across. Also include your menu, with an appetising picture of one of your dishes and perhaps even one of your recipes, so people have a reason to read your blog and share that post. Be sure to include your next menu and the event's date, with details of how people can book. Share this blog post across all your social media platforms.

Building on your client base

Email everyone who came to your last evening, thank them for attending, and give them the menu and details for the next event. Ask them to forward it on to their foodie friends if they're not able to make it. Try and get as many bookings in the bag as early on as possible – our pop-ups regularly sell out weeks in advance, and we usually have a reserve list, just in case someone cancels.

Are there other foodie events you could attend in your area to drum up support? We went to local food and drink festivals, had stalls at farmers' markets and William offered his services as a 'chef for hire' for the neighbourhood's dinner parties. For all of these we took business cards with our contact details and blog address on, so we could once again build up more customers.

Also, don't be afraid to ask people if they want to join your pop-up mailing list and jot down their details – this comes especially in handy if you have a last-minute cancellation as you have a ready-made bank of people to call on.

Once you've had a successful evening, you will find people are much more willing to come to the next one.

Long-term planning

Now you've held your first event, you will have a good idea of what you want from your pop-up restaurant experience. Is it an occasional fun hobby that you enjoy sharing with new people? Is it something you'd like to progress to a career change and turn it into more of a business? Or is it something you'd like to use as an extra revenue stream to help pay the bills each month on top of your day job?

Be clear on your goals, and let that dictate the direction you want to take your pop-up in from here. Use sections of this book again to help create your next pop-up or supper club adventure, which your added experience, understanding and heightened imagination can only make better than before. Remember, anything is possible; look at many of the successful restaurateurs we spoke to for this book whose projects started out as a one-off experiment with friends. Their passion and enthusiasm for creating an imaginative and exciting dining experience for food lovers is what has taken them to the dizzy heights of this country's food scene. And one thing is for sure, they have all made mistakes, they have all thrived on the pressures of the kitchen and none of them would ever step back into their life before running a restaurant and chasing that dream began.

CHAPTER 15

RECIPES
FOR SUCCESS

These foolproof recipes have become staples at our pop-up restaurants as they are lifesavers when you are time poor – often the case when you've got thirty covers to get out! You can adapt these meals using your own favourite ingredients, but remember not to over-complicate them – their beauty is in their simplicity.

The principles for these recipes are:

1. Dishes that can be prepared in advance
2. Dishes that can be kept warm or served cold
3. Dishes that are super quick to cook

We try to mix these in with one dish each time that's a little more taxing, so that William gets a chance to showcase his talents. Keep that in mind when you're putting together your menu, and you can't go far wrong!

All recipes serve six so multiply quantities as required.

Starters

Fortnum & Mason's French Onion Soup

This restaurant classic will help you out when timings are tight, as you prepare it in advance and simply keep it warm throughout the evening, heating up to piping hot just before serving. The only last-minute cooking is the French bread float you need to toast and grill for the garnish.

3 medium-sized white onions
A generous knob of salted butter
6 tsp Fortnum & Mason's beef extract (this is the magic
**   ingredient, so do not try to substitute!)**
1.5 litres/2½ pints water
Salt
Pepper
French bread
Parmesan or Gruyère

1. Peel and thinly slice the onions and place in a saucepan with the butter; brown off the onions over a medium heat. Keep stirring to make sure that the onions are evenly cooked off. Once done, add the Fortnum & Mason beef extract and stir to coat the onions. Stir for around 2–3 minutes then pour in the water.
2. Cover with a lid and simmer for around fifteen minutes. Season with salt and pepper to taste. Keep covered and warm until you're ready to serve, bringing it up to simmer again.
3. Serve with a float of French bread and grilled grated cheese on top (Gruyère is our favourite, but any hard cheese such as Parmesan will work). Do this by slicing French bread into 1-inch thick pieces, toast under the grill on both sides, float one slice of toast on top of each bowl of soup, sprinkle the float with grated cheese, and then place the whole bowl back under the grill for a minute or so to melt the cheese topping.

Duck Liver and Orange Pâté

Prepare this dish fully in advance and serve on the night with crisp French toast or artisan bread.

450g/16oz duck livers (these are cheaper bought from a butcher's than from a supermarket)
2 oranges
1 good-sized white onion
250g/9oz salted butter (a knob of this is used for frying)
Season to taste

1. Finely chop the onion and fry in a knob of butter, until soft. Add the livers and fry over a high heat for a couple of minutes until lightly browned on the outside, but still pink in the middle.
2. Place the contents of the frying pan in a food processor. Add the zest from one orange and its juice. Blitz until the livers are a fine paste, and add salt and pepper to season.
3. Line a small bread tin or ceramic terrine with cling film and spoon the mixture in.
4. Melt the remaining butter in a saucepan over a low heat, separate the butter solids off and throw them away, retaining only the clarified butter.
5. Slice the remaining orange thinly and lay four slices over the top of the pâté.
6. Pour the melted, clarified butter on top until it just covers the orange slices.
7. Leave to cool on the sideboard for about an hour, then place in the fridge to set for 12 hours. Slice before serving with toast or bread and a homemade chutney.

Smoked Duck and Quail's Egg Salad

You will need a smoker for this recipe – a fantastic investment for any budding chef – or you could replace the duck with any good quality deli-bought smoked meat if you don't have one. All the individual elements of this dish are prepared in advance, so all that remains for you to do is assemble the colourful and impressive salads as your guests arrive!

For the soft-boiled quail's eggs
24 quail's eggs

For the smoked duck breasts
3 duck breasts
Maldon sea salt
Oak-smoked wood chips

For the dressing
2 bags of rocket salad
1 punnet of cherry tomatoes
2 tbsp honey
2 tbsp balsamic vinegar
2 tbsp olive oil
Maldon sea salt
Black pepper

For the smoked duck breasts
(Cook these two days before your event.)
1. Liberally coat the flesh side of the duck breasts with Maldon sea salt. Place these on a plate in the fridge to cure for about 3 hours.
2. Remove the breasts and pat them down with a piece of kitchen paper so they are dry, as the salt will have drawn out much of the moisture.
3. Place a few handfuls of the wood chips in the smoker and heat it to around 77°C. Place your duck breasts inside and smoke for about 2 hours.

4. When done, which you can tell because the meat will become slightly firm, remove the breasts from the smoker, allow them to cool and then chill in the fridge.

For the soft-boiled quail's eggs
(Cook these the afternoon of your event.)

1. Bring a pan of water, with a little salt, to the boil. Gently add your quail's eggs, keeping the water on a rolling boil and time for exactly 1½ minutes. When the time is up, remove quickly from the heat and hold the pan underneath a running cold tap to stop the eggs cooking.
2. When the eggs are cool to handle (this should take about 2–3 minutes) they are ready to peel – you will need patience here and a gentle touch.
3. Once peeled, pop them in the fridge and cover with cling film, ready for your evening.

For the dressing
(Mix on the afternoon of your event.)
Mix together the balsamic vinegar, honey and olive oil. Season with salt and pepper.

To assemble your salad
1. Place a handful of rocket on each plate with some cherry tomatoes, halved and salted.
2. Thinly slice half a duck breast and scatter over the salad.
3. Cut around five quail's eggs, place on the salad and then drizzle with the honey and balsamic dressing.

Mains

Rib Buster with Chantenay Carrots and New-Season Broccoli

This flavoursome and relatively cheap cut of beef is great to cook for a large number of people, as you cook it for an hour and then can leave it to rest, simply carving off slices as and when you need them.

Time it so that you remove the beef from the oven when your guests arrive, so all that remains for you to do to this dish is cook your vegetables and make a quick gravy. This joint is called 'rib buster' because, while roasting in your oven, it will expand rather than contract as most joints do, but your supermarket or butcher will probably call it short ribs.

1kg/2 lb 3oz joint of rib buster beef
500g/1 lb 1oz Chantenay carrots
500g/1 lb 1oz of tender stem broccoli
1 tbsp plain flour
Salt
Pepper
1 glass of good red wine
2 tbsp crab apple jelly
1 tsp cornflour (if needed)

1. Preheat oven to 220°C. Season the joint with a rub of flour seasoned with salt and pepper. Seal any cut ends on a hot frying pan, until browned. Lay the joint on a roasting tray and pop in a hot oven for an hour.
2. When you slice into it, it should still be pink, fleshy and tender inside, with a golden-brown crust on the outside. Once done, remove from the oven, place on a carving board, cover with tin foil and leave for 20 minutes (as your guests are seated and enjoying their starters).

3. While the meat is resting, boil a pan of water, and add to that Chantenay carrots and new-season broccoli, to simmer for about 10 minutes.

4. While these are cooking, make a gravy with the juices from the beef, by adding the wine and crab apple jelly to the roasting tin and placing over a low heat. Keep stirring until the gravy has reduced; season and add a teaspoon of cornflour, if you'd like it thicker, or a little of the water from your vegetables if you want to thin it out.

Lemon-Roasted Spatchcock Poussin with Rosemary

This dish can be sitting ready for you to pop in the oven once your guests are tucking into their starters. A poussin is a small chicken and you will be able to find it in any butcher's or supermarket. If you are unsure how to spatchcock a bird, ask your butcher to do this for you, as it's a relatively complicated process for amateur chefs.

3 lemons
225g/8oz salted butter
6 sprigs of rosemary, plus 5–6 extra leaves
6 spatchcocked poussin

For the salad
Honey
Lemons
Olive oil

1. In a blender, blitz together the juice of one lemon and the butter with a few rosemary leaves.
2. Using your fingers, rub this rosemary and butter mix into the skin and flesh of the birds. Place them in a large roasting tin with a sprig of rosemary on each, and a couple of slices of the second lemon over each bird.
3. Preheat oven to 200°C and when hot, pop the birds in the tin in for 25 minutes.
4. You will be able to tell they are cooked by cutting through the skin on the back of one bird and sliding a knife a little way along – if the juices run clear, then leave the bird to rest for a few minutes, while you dress the plates with a fresh seasonal salad.
5. Make a honey and lemon dressing for the salad by mixing 2 tbsp each of honey, lemon juice and olive oil, and season. This can also be prepared before the night.

Grouse and Coconut Curry

Curry is fantastic for pop-ups or supper clubs as you can cook this in large quantities fairly easily and it can be simmering away in the background during the first course. You don't have to use grouse – any dark meat will do, such as beef, pheasant, venison, lamb or even goat! Because it works so well with game, we tend to cook this curry in the autumn when we also have a glut of fresh, in-season beef tomatoes, which help create the delicious juicy sauce. Curry often tastes best on its second day, so feel free to cook this up the day before and simply warm it up as you cook the naan and rice.

2 brace of grouse (or 1.5kg/3 lb 5oz of alternative dark meat, suggested above)
4 good-sized onions (red or white)
50g/2 oz extra virgin coconut oil
6 cloves of garlic
2 thumbs of fresh ginger
2 tbsp garam masala
4 tbsp medium curry powder
1.5kg/3 lb 5oz beef tomatoes
4 carrots (grated)
2 cans coconut milk
1 small pot of crème fraîche

1. Pluck the grouse, remove the breasts and chop the meat into cubes. Put to one side. Alternatively, if you are not using game bird meat, dice up the beef, lamb, venison or goat.
2. Finely chop the onions and sweat them down in a frying pan over a high heat in the extra virgin coconut oil. Add the six chopped cloves of garlic and the thumbs of diced fresh ginger.
3. Once the onions have cooked to a soft golden brown, add your diced meat and move around the pan with a wooden spoon so the meat is sealed in the delicious seasonings.

4. After 5 minutes, add the garam masala and medium curry powder and, again, move the meat around the pan with the wooden spoon to coat the meat with these spices.
5. Add the freshly chopped beef tomatoes and simmer, uncovered, for five minutes, then add the grated carrots and pour in the coconut milk.
6. Simmer uncovered until the sauce has reduced by half (this takes around 30–45 minutes).
7. Serve with fluffy rice, naan bread or fresh noodles, and a big dollop of crème fraîche. Abigail loves a boiled egg, sliced banana and mango chutney to accompany this curry, but William prefers it served simply as it is.

Tomato, Basil and Parmesan Risotto

This is a great little vegetarian main for serving at pop-ups and supper clubs because it can be cooked mostly in advance, and finished off just in time for service. Because it requires quite a bit of attention in the cooking, being continually stirred, we find that this method of advanced cooking helps minimise risk in a stressful kitchen!

6 shallots
Knob of salted butter
400g/14oz arborio rice
3 litres vegetable stock
1kg/2 lb 3oz fresh tomatoes
Handful of fresh basil leaves
150g/5oz Parmesan

1. Finely chop the shallots and fry them in the butter in a large saucepan over a medium heat until they start to turn a golden brown. Add the rice and, continually stirring, fry for a few minutes. Add 500ml of vegetable stock and continue to stir, making sure nothing sticks to the bottom of the pan.
2. After around five minutes, add the chopped tomatoes and carry on stirring.
3. After 10 minutes (or when the rice starts to look dry again) add another 500ml of stock. Keep stirring until the rice looks dry again, then add another 500ml of stock, and the chopped basil leaves.
4. After a further five minutes, test the rice between your teeth to see if it is cooked. If you're planning to reheat the risotto later, when you bite the rice it should have a very slightly floury centre. If you're planning to serve directly, it should be soft all the way through so always test again just before serving. If the rice has not yet reached the correct

consistency, continue to add stock until it has been cooked to the correct stage.

5. When reheating your risotto you will need to add some more stock and reheat for 5–10 minutes, to turn it from floury to soft just before service. Serve dressed with a dusting of Parmesan and a sprinkling of basil.

Mini Stuffed Pumpkins

This is an impressive-looking dish to serve to any vegetarians and is best in autumn, when all the ingredients are in season, so taste their best. The filling for these can be cooked in the afternoon, with the pumpkin 'pots' pre-stuffed, then roasted on the night. It's the perfect choice for a Halloween pop-up!

1.5kg/3 lb 5oz of a mixture of aubergines, tomatoes, mushrooms, peppers, carrots and red onions
Olive oil
Salt
Pepper
6 mini pumpkins
Worcestershire sauce
Goat's cheese (optional)

1. Coarsely chop the vegetables (apart from the pumpkins), place in a roasting tray and pour a good glug of olive oil over them (around 5 tbsp), season with salt and pepper and a few dashes of Worcestershire sauce. Toss the vegetables in this dressing and roast in the oven at 130°C for an hour, turning them every 20 minutes or so to stop them sticking to the bottom of the tray. You will be able to tell when the vegetables are cooked as they will have shrunk and turned soft. Remove the tray from the oven and leave to cool.

2. Cut off a plug-shaped hole from the top of each mini pumpkin, spoon out its centre and discard the fleshy inside. Keep the lids as these will be used to top off your mini pumpkins.

3. Take your empty pumpkin pots and stuff them with the cold vegetables. This is now all your prep done!

4. Around 45 minutes before you want to serve the pumpkins, place them in a hot oven at around 180°C with the lids on.

5. If you want to add cheese, a couple of minutes before the pumpkins are ready to serve, remove the lids and place a few slices of goat's cheese on the top of the vegetables, put the lids back on and pop them in the oven until the cheese begins to bubble and melt.
6. To serve, place them in the centre of a plate, with a side of crusty bread and butter, and a spoon.

Pan-Fried Sea Bass with Burnt Butter

With fish, more than any other foodstuff, it's the quality of the ingredient that speaks for itself, so don't scrimp on the sea bass! A simple burnt butter sauce is all that is needed to offset this firm white meatily textured fish. It's a dish that you can flash fry and will be ready for the table in under 10 minutes. There are only three main ingredients, but it's still easy to ruin if you leave it for too long, so make sure you are fully prepped and are not going to be interrupted for around 15 minutes once you start cooking.

225g/8 oz butter
6 fillets of sea bass – use small whole fish fillets, not steaks
1 lemon
Salt
Pepper

1. Melt the butter in a large frying pan over a medium heat. Test it is hot enough to cook by putting a drop of water in the pan – it should sizzle.
2. When the pan is ready, place the sea bass skin side down into the sizzling butter. The fillets will curl and move a little if they are fresh – this is fine! Tip the pan to one side and using a large spoon ladle the sizzling butter over the fish. Cook like this for around 5 minutes until the fish feels firm when you prod it gently.
3. Serve on a plate with a little of the burnt butter sauce spooned over the fish, with a squeeze of one lemon wedge, and season with a little salt and pepper.

Dauphinoise Potatoes

Dauphinoise potatoes work as a fantastic side dish to accompany the burnt butter sea bass and, once again, can be prepared well in advance – just pop a casserole dish of them in the oven for 45 minutes on the night.

8 large Maris Piper potatoes
1 white onion
1 pint double cream
1 pint milk
3 cloves of garlic
100g/3.5oz Gruyère cheese

1. Thinly slice your potatoes and onion. Place your cream, milk and crushed garlic in a saucepan and simmer. Add your potato and onions to the pan and simmer for 4 minutes.
2. Remove the onions and potatoes with a spoon and layer them into a casserole dish. Remove the crushed garlic from the milk mixture; pour the pan's contents over the potatoes and onions in your casserole dish. Scatter the grated Gruyère over the top.
3. To cook on the evening, bake in a preheated oven at 190ºC for 45 minutes, until the potato is cooked to a soft golden brown.

Sweets

Tarte Tatin

This delicious warm dessert is quick to pull together at the end of the night. Its combination of juicy sweet fruit, crunchy caramel and golden, buttery puff pastry will make a fantastic finale to any dinner. If you have an abundance of time you could make the puff pastry for this yourself, but shop-bought puff pastry is one of those rare items that, unless you're a trained pastry chef, is hard to beat.

1 pack of ready-to-roll puff pastry
4 sweet red apples
1 jar of good quality plum jam
1 egg

1. Preheat oven to around 180ºC. Roll out the puff pastry into a rectangle. Trim 1.5cm off all the way around the rectangle, to create the sides of your tart.
2. Beat the egg in a bowl to make a wash and, using a pastry brush, dab the offcuts with some egg wash and glue them to the edges of your tart base to make a ridge all the way around its outside. Don't forget to prick the base of your pastry case, otherwise it will rise.
3. Finely cut your apples into slices and lay these all over the tart's base. Pour the jar of plum jam evenly over the apples and put in the hot oven until golden brown – this should take around 12 minutes, but keep an eye on it as it can burn easily.
4. Serve with clotted cream.

Caramelised Poached Oranges

This is without a doubt one of the simplest desserts you can make, but it tastes spectacular! The ingredients are also super cheap, so will allow you the chance to splash out on more expensive ingredients earlier on in the menu. We are willing to bet half your guests will insist this dish is steeped in booze because of its delicious, syrupy flavours – but you will know the truth!

6 large oranges
450g/1 lb granulated sugar
½ pint of water
Some crystallised orange peel
A small tub of good quality vanilla ice cream (those of you more confident can make your own)

1. Peel the oranges with a small sharp knife, making sure you remove all the fiddly bits of white bitter pith. Cut the peeled oranges in half, across the grain of the orange (so, perpendicular to the segments).
2. Place the sugar and water in a deep frying pan and bring it gently to the boil, stirring every few minutes.
3. When all the sugar has dissolved, place the orange halves, flat side down, in the syrup and cook for around 8 minutes, checking constantly that the sugar doesn't burn. If the syrup gets too thick, add a little more water.
4. When cooked, plate up the oranges and drizzle the syrup over them while still warm. Garnish with some crystallised orange peel and a kernel of ice cream (place a metal spoon in hot water before scooping the ice cream to help shape it into an elegant 'almond'). Serve immediately.

Brandy Snaps with Moonshine Cream

This recipe was popular at our pop-up speakeasy. We used sloe gin because we had an abundance of that at home, but any liqueur such as brandy or Cointreau would do. Cook the brandy snaps and make the moonshine cream in advance of your evening, and store them in airtight containers. Then all that remains for you to do is pipe the cream in just before serving to stop the biscuit coating going soggy.

For the brandy snaps
115g/4oz salted butter
115g/4oz golden syrup
115g/4oz caster sugar
115g/4oz plain flour
½ tsp ground ginger
Juice of ½ lemon

For the moonshine cream
280ml/½ pint cold double cream
2 tbsp sloe gin (or other liqueur)

Garnish
Six halved plums (optional)

1. Preheat the oven to 175ºC.
2. Place the butter, syrup and sugar in a pan over heat until they melt together. Then add the flour, ginger and lemon juice, and stir.
3. Keep this mixture warm and line two baking trays with greaseproof baking paper. Spoon small blobs of the mixture (about the size of a large marble) onto the baking parchment, leaving plenty of space between each blob, as they spread out as they cook.
4. Pop into the oven, in batches, for around 8–10 minutes, keeping a close eye on them. They must be golden brown, but not too dark as this will make them taste burnt and bitter.

5. While still warm, remove from the baking parchment with a palette knife and roll each brandy snap sheet around the handle of a wooden spoon greased with butter. As it starts to harden, slide it off the spoon.

6. Prepare your cream by whipping it in the mixer, and slowly pouring in the sloe gin (or your liqueur of choice). Adding it gradually will help make sure the cream doesn't split. Pop in an airtight container in the fridge and pipe into the brandy snaps just before serving. We garnished ours with ripe, sliced plums to complement the plummy flavour of the sloes.

CHECKLISTS

Here's a list of what you need to have in place when you run your pop-up, supper club or bar. It doesn't have to be followed in order and not all items on the list are absolutely essential, as every pop-up is different, but it's a good basic template to make sure all your bases are covered. Adapt it to your unique evening and you will be sure to skyrocket to success.

Pop-up restaurant or supper club checklist

- Venue booked (if needed)
- Temporary Events Notice applied for (at least twenty-one days in advance) if you're selling alcohol
- Menu chosen
- Poster designed
- Publicity campaign launched
- Furniture and kitchen equipment organised
- Staff booked and briefed (if needed)
- Risk assessment carried out
- Food hygiene course completed
- Insurance taken out
- Payment taken, or if paying on the night, float and card payment equipment organised
- Menus printed
- Ingredients ordered/bought
- Venue cleaned
- Venue set up
- Equipment checked
- Food prep done
- Open for business!

Pop-up bar checklist

- Venue booked
- Music/entertainment organised
- Temporary Events Notice applied for (at least twenty-one days in advance)
- Furniture and bar equipment organised
- Glasses ordered
- Stock ordered
- Publicity launched
- Staff booked and briefed
- Insurance taken out
- Risk assessment carried out
- Drinks and snacks menus printed
- Venue cleaned
- Venue set up
- Staff trained
- All bar equipment checked
- Open for business!

APPENDIX 2
USEFUL CONTACTS

For legal advice on starting a small business

The Federation of Small Businesses helps its members by offering advice on health and safety and your legal requirements as a small business owner. It can also help with financial guidance and provides the opportunity for you to meet with other small local business owners. This could help raise the profile of your pop-up and offer you the chance to team up with other people. This could also be a good place to find out about potential empty venues.

www.fsb.org.uk

For advice on running a food business

The Food Standards Agency has lots of helpful information on setting up a food business and what your legal requirements are. It also explains how to contact your local authority, register your pop-up restaurant and features a checklist for starting up.

www.food.gov.uk

For legal advice on being an employer

This site explains in simple terms where you stand in relation to the law regarding the different types of workers and their rights, health and safety, recruiting staff and minimum wage. Take a look at www.gov.uk/browse/employing-people.

For advice on health and safety, risk assessment and alcohol licensing

There is plenty of guidance on the Health and Safety Executive's website regarding how to carry out a risk assessment for a small catering venture. There are handy templates to help you through the process and details about how to apply for a Personal Licence and a Temporary Events Notice.

www.hse.gov.uk

For investment in your pop-up

The following crowdfunding sites are all worth taking a look at if you're searching for investment in your business:

- www.fundingtree.co.uk
- www.fundingcircle.com
- www.crowdfunder.co.uk
- www.crowdcube.com
- www.seedrs.com

For advice on grants and funding

Good sites where you can apply for funding and grants include:

- www.lotterygoodcauses.org.uk
- www.grantnet.com
- www.gov.uk/apply-funding-community-project

There are also lottery grants awards for small community projects across the UK.

- http://www.biglotteryfund.org.uk/funding/awards-for-all

For pop-up and supper club insurance

Insurance companies specialising in providing cover for supper clubs, pop-ups and underground restaurants include:

- www.simplybusiness.co.uk
- www.penninsure.co.uk

To find pop-up restaurant spaces

Pop-Up Space

This is the UK's first property consultancy specialising in finding pop-up spaces and can help organise pop-up insurance.

- www.popupspace.com

We Are Pop-Up

Search spaces for pop-up hire across the UK.

- www.wearepopup.com

The Empty Shops Network

A site that aims to help people reduce, reuse and recycle empty shops and other spaces in towns and cities.

- www.emptyshopsnetwork.co.uk

3space

3space works in partnership with landlords and leaseholders to offer organisations that benefit the community temporary free-of-charge access to otherwise empty properties across the UK for pop-up projects.

- www.3space.org

40 Alfred Place
A 40-seat fully licensed restaurant in Bristol available for hire for pop-up restaurants.

• www.40alfredplace.net

The Meanwhile Organisation
Using property temporarily to help bring about change in neighbourhoods to make something happen that is good for the area and its people.

• www.meanwhile.org.uk

Research pop-up restaurants and supper clubs

Pop-up Space blog
A smart little blog with the latest news from the world of pop-ups.

• www.popupspaceblog.com

Find a supper club
A great blog site for finding supper clubs, pop-up restaurants and underground restaurants across the country with lots of advice on insurance and a healthy forum exchanging advice and recipes.

• www.supperclubfangroup.ning/com

The London Foodie
A site which reviews London's restaurants, supper clubs and hotels, wine tastings, written by supper club host Luiz Hara.

• www.thelondonfoodie.co.uk

Grub club

Grub club lets foodies know where pop-up chefs are appearing across London.

- www.grubclub.com

Square Meal

A reviews website featuring some of the country's best pop-ups.

- www.squaremeal.co.uk

The London Street Foodie

A great blog reviewing pop-up street food stalls written by the food editor of the *Evening Standard*, Victoria Stewart.

- www.londonstreetfoodie.co.uk

Further reading

Pop-Up Business For Dummies by Dan Thompson (John Wiley & Sons, 2012) is a fantastic read on starting a pop-up business in general.

INDEX